ALL IN GOOD TIME

ALL IN GOOD TIME

One hundred menus for advance preparation

by Angela Kay

LONDON
GEORGE ALLEN & UNWIN LTD · RUSKIN HOUSE · MUSEUM STREET

First published in 1972

ISBN 0 04 641029 5 Paperback

Printed in Great Britain
by Butler & Tanner Ltd
Frome and London

To Mummy, with love

Foreword

This is a book of menus, recipes and food ideas for small dinner parties and week-end cooking. It has been specially designed for those whose time in the kitchen is broken up—perhaps by a job or the demands of small children. Or, for those who simply prefer to spend their week-ends relaxing with husbands, families or hobbies, yet still want to be able to delight and surprise their guests with unusual, thoughtful dishes.

There are many recipes which, with the help of a refrigerator or really cold larder and close-sealing plastic containers, may be brought close—if not right up—to the finishing post the day before the party.

It is always hard to know how much preparation may be safely done in advance and this book is designed to detail this very thoroughly. The 'advance' part of each recipe may be quickly and easily distinguished from the rest because it is printed in red. So, if a hostess knows that the dinner party day itself is going to be very hectic, then she may select recipes printed completely in red and prepare the entire meal the day before. With the reassuring thought that her work is done she may then spend D-day attending the school prize-giving, planting out the wallflowers or having a facial.

Not *every* recipe in this book may be prepared in advance, but because of the 'red and black' system, you can see at a glance what must be left until the last moment and plan accordingly. So, if you find that you have a spare half hour between finishing the ironing and collecting the children from school, you know that you can hardboil the eggs for tomorrow's Egg Mousse, prepare the vinaigrette dressing for the salad, or make the Avocado Soup. And all this in the sure knowledge that nothing will suffer from having been prepared a day early.

Quantities given in the recipes are for four persons.

STORING AND REHEATING 'ADVANCE-COOKED' FOOD

To advance-cook with complete confidence you must have a refrigerator or very cold larder. Our climate is temperate, but does throw in the occasional thunderstorm, guaranteed to upset an unprotected potato-based soup or creamy pudding.

Plastic containers with really airtight lids are ideal for storing pre-cooked foods or raw, but prepared vegetables and saladstuffs. Foil and plastic film are also useful as added protection for casseroles or pans whose lids do not fit very snugly.

Reheating should be done gently, with fairly constant stirring or supervision to prevent burning or overcooking. Soups and sauces should be stirred over a low flame; casseroles should be placed in a preheated moderate oven until heated through. Salad dressings and vinaigrettes should be stored in glass jars or bottles with screw tops, then shaken vigorously just before use. Mayonnaise should be stored in glass, pottery or plastic containers at the bottom of the refrigerator, and allowed to rest at room temperature for half an hour before use.

Even food to be served cold—with the exception of ice cream—should be removed from the refrigerator or cold larder a few minutes before it is to be served, otherwise the flavour is not allowed to develop fully.

ABBREVIATIONS

tbs	= tablespoonful		hot oven	= 400°–450°F	= 205°–232°C
tsp	= teaspoonful		moderate oven	= 300°–350°F	= 150°–177°C
dess	= dessertspoonful		low oven	= 250°–300°F	= 121°–149°C

CONVERSION TABLE

1 gram	=	·035 oz
28·35 gram	=	1 oz
100 gram	=	3½ oz
114 gram	=	4 oz (approx)
226·78 gram	=	½ lb
500 gram	=	1 lb 1½ oz (approx)

1 kilogram	=	2·21 lb
1 decilitre	=	3½ fl. oz
½ litre	=	17½ fl. oz or a generous ¾ pint
1 litre	=	1¾ pints

Menu Contents

33
Green Pea Soup
Fillet Steaks with Croûtons
French Beans with Tomatoes
Chocolate Brandy Whip

34
Flamiche
Pork Chops with Cranberries
Cabbage and Tomato Salad
Melon Salad

35
Stuffed Eggs
Pheasant with Celery and Cream
French Beans with Mushrooms
Creamy Cherry Flan

36
Mushroom Salad
Gammon Cooked in Sherry
Red Cabbage with Apple
Caramel Ice Cream

37
Split Pea Soup
Côtelettes d'Agneau en Papillotes
Asparagus with Lemon Sauce
Fresh Figs

38
Smoked Trout Pâté
Meat Loaf with Egg
Globe Artichokes with Butter
Apple Cream

39
Avocado with Chives and Vinaigrette
Cidered Ham
Stuffed Aubergines
Redcurrant Mousse

40
Stuffed Tomatoes
Escalopes de Veau à la Crème aux Champignons
Gratin de Grenoble
Strawberries with Rum Cream

41
Prawn Cocktail
Beef Olives
Bean Purée
Orange Pudding

42
Soupe Catalane
Roast Pork with Orange
Roast Parsnips
Baked Apple with Yogurt

43
Creamed Eggs on Garlic Toast
Polpette
September Salad
Hot Fruit Salad

44
Cream of Chicken Soup
Rôti de Porc Boulangère
Tomatoes in Cream Sauce
Lemon Whip

45
Dressed Crab with Avocado
Navarin Printanier
Parslied Rice
Apple Fool

46
Crudités with Garlic Mayonnaise
Chicken Sauté Archiduc
Courgettes and Onions
Biscuit Cake

47
Germiny Soup
Veal Flambé
Beans with Celery
Apple and Blackcurrant Miroton

48
Cream Cheese with Crispies
Beef and Onion Goulash
Cucumber and Chive Salad
Lemon Cake

49
Bressane Mushroom Soup
Escalopes de Veau à la Crème
Lemon Leeks
Mincemeat Crumble

50
Aubergine Fritters
Irish Stew
Sweetcorn with Herb Butter
Gooseberry Fool

51
French Bean and Prawn Salad
Veal Paprika
Purple Broccoli with Lemon Butter
Pear Fool

52
Onions with Vinaigrette Sauce
Calf's Kidneys in Vodka
Marrow in Butter
Chestnut Snow

53
Mushroom Soup
Casserole de Boeuf Dauphinoise
Rice with Almonds and Raisins
Grapefruit Cream

54
Baked Mushrooms
Mexican Chicken Casserole
Spaghetti with Green Butter
Hawaiian Ice

55
Tomato Soup
Lamb Casserole with Chestnuts
Cabbage with Nutmeg
Italian Syllabub

56
Jambon aux Oeufs
Fillet Steaks, Sauce Belge
Israeli Salad
Strawberry Crème Brûlée

57
Tuna Fish Pâté
Wine Baked Veal
Leeks and Tomatoes
Stuffed Peaches

58
Sweetcorn with Butter
Strogoulash
Tomates Provençales en Salade
Marmince Pie

59
Curried Parsnip Soup
Fricandeau of Veal
Casseroled Spring Greens
Apricot Crusts

60
Marinaded Kippers
Stuffed Green Peppers
Mixed Salad
Strawberry Fool

61
Mushroom, Cucumber and French Bean Sal
Roast Stuffed Leg of Lamb
Baked Beetroot in Cream
Rhubarb Crumble

62
Spring Soup
Braised Beef with Prunes
Casseroled Potatoes
Cheese with Fruit

63
Portuguese Sardines
Roast Grouse with White Grapes
Peas with Cream
Cream Cheese and Chestnut

64
Carrot and Watercress Soup
Scaloppine Pizzaiuola
Swedish Potatoes
Gâteau Malakoff

65
Sweet Pepper and Olive Salad
Steak, Kidney and Mushrooms
Jerusalem Artichokes
Pots au Chocolat

66
Jerusalem Artichoke Soup
Escalopes with Black Olives
Green Salad
Chocolate and Orange Mousse

67
Spanish Omelette
Meat Loaf with Cream Sauce
French Bean Salad
Pineapple Baskets

68
Lentil Soup
Noisettes d'Agneau en Brochette
Globe Artichokes with Vinaigrette
Strawberries with Orange

69
Oeufs en Cocotte
Beef and Potato Goulash
Avocado and Cucumber Salad
Rummy Apples

70
Onion Soup
Ham Loaf
Artichokes in Tomato Juice
Christmas Ice Cream

71
Eggs with Skordalia
Red Mullet 'Foiled'
French Beans with Cream
Kay Fruit Salad

72
Chiffonade
Steak and Pimento Pie
Mixed Cucumber Salad
Charlotte Russe

73
Curried Aubergines
Veal with Pineapple
Foiled Onions
Vanilla Mousse

74
Quiche Lorraine
Gigot d'Agneau à la Provençale
Cucumber and Cream Salad
Greek Fruit Salad

75
Potato Soup with Celeriac
Boeuf Stroganoff
Cauliflower with Onions
Pineapple and Orange Salad

76
Potage Véronique
Veal with Cream and Cucumber
Carottes à la Vichy
Brown Bread Ice Cream

77
Prawns with Baked Eggs
Turkish Pilaff
Pepper and Olive Salad
Camille Fruits

78
Shrimp and Cucumber Soup
Pork with Coriander
Jacket Potatoes
Cream Cheese Cake

79
Oeufs à la Neige
Daube à la Corsoise
Polish Cauliflower
Atholl Brose

80
Smoked Trout Quiche
Chicken Pilaff
Chicory and Watercress Salad
Layered Apples

81
Chilled Avocado Soup
Paupiettes of Beef
Aubergine Purée
Baked Apricots

82
Hungarian Salad
Cornish Pasties
Courgettes and Tomatoes
Bananas with Rum and Cream

83
Croûte au Jambon
Brazilian Poussins
Stuffed Tomatoes
Lemon Ice Cream

84
Carrot and Orange Soup
Pork and Prunes
Cabbage and Cream
Viennese Biscuit Cake

85
Mushrooms en Croûte
Devilled Cutlets
Cabbage with Cheese Sauce
Greek Egg Custard

86
Mixed Fruit Juice
Kidney, Pork and Bean Hotpot
Tomato Salad with Cream
Creamy Apple Flan

87
Creamy Onion Soup
Duck with Cherries
Risotto
Whipped Cream Roll

88
Prawn and Egg Mousse
Portuguese Fillet of Pork
Grilled Garlic Tomatoes
Greek Yogurt

89
Grapefruit and Orange Salad
Provençal Beef Stew
Macaroni Milano
Chocolate and Chestnut

90
Tomato and Orange Soup
Lamb Fricassée with Lettuce
Sprouts with Walnuts
Apple Omelette

91
Tomato Mousse
Medaillons in Mandelrock
Carrots with Parsley Sauce
Almond Apples

92
Eggs with Dill Sauce
Stuffed Kidneys
Fried Onion Rings
Stuffed Oranges

93
Pea Soup with Bacon
Escalopes de Veau en Aillade
Onions Topped with Cream
Rhubarb Sponge

94
Tuna and Almond Salad
Filet de Boeuf Flambé à l'Avignonnaise
Leeks and Mushrooms
Eastern Oranges

95
Avocado and Prawn Mayonnaise
Lamb Cutlets with Mint Butter
Chicory with Cheese Sauce
Gooseberry Ice Cream

96
Tomatoed Prawns
Hotpot
Spinach with Cheese
Apple Flan

97
Parsnip Mayonnaise
Roast Pork with Lemon
Cabbage with Caraway
Stuffed Prunes

98
Oranged Melon
Chicken and Aubergine Casserole
Swiss Potatoes
Cheesecake

99
Lettuce and Onion Soup
Cod Provençale
Raw Mushroom Salad
Banana Trifle

100
Egg and Tomato Mayonnaise
Chicken with Orange
Carrot Purée
Brown Bread Cream

ORANGE AND OLIVE SALAD

4 large oranges
4 tbs olive oil
1 tbs vinegar
4 oz black olives
salt, pepper
watercress and chicory

Blend together the oil, vinegar, salt and finely grated rind of 2 oranges. Peel the oranges very carefully, discarding all pith. Slice the oranges into thin rounds and arrange them in a large shallow dish, without overlapping if possible. Pour over the orange and oil dressing. Sprinkle with a fine layer of freshly milled black pepper. Chill for 2–3 hours before serving on a bed of watercress and chicory.

FILET DE PORC EN CROUTE

1 lb pork fillet
salt, pepper
2 oz lean boiled ham
1 egg
1 lb puff pastry
1 oz butter

for duxelles:
1 lb button mushrooms
1 large onion
2 oz butter
salt, pepper
thyme
2 tbs chopped parsley
4 tbs fresh breadcrumbs
2 eggs

First, prepare the duxelles by tossing the finely chopped mushrooms and onion in butter for 5 minutes. Season to taste with salt, pepper and chopped thyme. Fold in the parsley, breadcrumbs and beaten eggs. Mix thoroughly over a low flame for a few minutes, then allow the mixture to cool. Meanwhile, season the pork fillet with salt and pepper. Heat the butter in a frying pan, and sear the pork all over in this. Allow it to cool. Roll out the pastry, about 10 inches wide, and 2–3 inches longer than the fillet. Place the fillet in the centre of the pastry, arrange the 'duxelles' on top, then cover with strips of boiled ham. Fold one side of the pastry over the fillet, paint it with beaten egg, then fold over the second half of pastry, to overlap the first. Cover the whole surface with more beaten egg, prick it lightly with a fork, and bake in a moderate oven for 40 minutes.

GLOBE ARTICHOKES WITH LEMON MAYONNAISE

4 globe artichokes
salt, pepper
1 lemon
½ pint mayonnaise

Trim the artichoke stalks. Bring to the boil a large panful of salted water. Add the artichokes and bring back to the boil. Allow to simmer until the artichokes are cooked. This will vary, of course, according to the size of the artichokes, but should take between 25–35 minutes. The artichoke is cooked when a leaf can be detached cleanly and easily. To the mayonnaise add the grated rind of ½ lemon and the strained juice of the whole lemon. This will produce a very sharp, rather runny mayonnaise which contrasts well with the artichoke. The quantity of lemon rind and juice can be adjusted, of course, according to how lemony a sauce is required.

COFFEE MALAKOFF

6 oz castor sugar
8 oz cakecrumbs or white breadcrumbs
8 oz unsalted butter
¾ gill black coffee
1 gill whipped cream
flaked almonds

Cream together the butter and sugar. Moisten the cakecrumbs or breadcrumbs with the black coffee. Add the creamed butter and sugar and mix well. Transfer the mixture to a serving dish and allow it to stand in a cool place for 1 hour. Cover with a layer of whipped cream and sprinkle with flaked almonds before serving.

SHRIMP SOUP

1 oz butter
1 carrot
1 onion
1 stick celery
1 leek
½ lb peeled shrimps
½ gill white wine or sherry
1 tbs brandy
1 pint basic white sauce
2 tbs double cream
watercress

Heat the butter in a thick pan. Add the chopped carrot, onion, celery and leek, using only the white part. Allow to cook gently until the vegetables are soft, but not coloured, then add the shrimps, keeping back a few to garnish each serving. Stir well, then add the wine. Warm the brandy (a soup ladle is a useful utensil for this process), pour it over the shrimps and set it alight. Allow to cook gently for 5 minutes, then liquidize or press the mixture through a sieve. Blend in the white sauce and reheat gently. Allow to simmer for 20 minutes, stirring from time to time. Strain the soup. **Just before serving, stir in the cream. Top each serving with a few shrimps and sprigs of watercress.**

PAUPIETTES OF VEAL

4 veal escalopes
4 slices lean boiled ham
4 oz fresh breadcrumbs
3 onions
salt, pepper
parsley
½ oz arrowroot
1½ gills beef stock
2 oz butter
2 carrots

Peel and finely chop 1 onion. Heat 1 oz butter in a frying pan, and fry the onion in this until soft, but not brown. Blend in the breadcrumbs and 1 tbs finely chopped parsley. Spread some of this mixture on each escalope, cover with a slice of boiled ham, then roll up each escalope and tie it securely. Heat a little more butter in the frying pan, and toss the rolled escalopes quickly in this until brown all over. Transfer them to an ovenware dish. Fry the remaining onions, peeled and chopped, and the finely sliced carrots in the butter for a few minutes, then add them to the veal. Add the boiling stock, cover with a lid and cook in a moderate oven for 1–1½ hours. **Dissolve the arrowroot in a little cold water. Blend in a little of the hot veal sauce. Stir well, then pour this over the paupiettes, and return to the oven for a final 5 minutes.**

RATATOUILLE

1 gill olive oil
2 onions
1 green pepper
3 courgettes
1 large aubergine
4 large tomatoes
2 cloves garlic
salt, pepper
thyme
bay leaf
parsley

Heat ½ gill oil in a thick pan. Add the peeled, sliced onions and allow to cook gently until soft and lightly browned. Add the peeled and finely chopped garlic and allow to cook for a further 5 minutes, then add the skinned and chopped tomatoes and the pimentoes, cut into small strips. In a second pan heat the remaining oil. Fry the sliced aubergines and sliced courgettes in this until tender. Blend together the two mixtures. Add plenty of salt and pepper, and the sprig of thyme, bay leaf and parsley, all tied together. Allow to simmer for a further 15 minutes. **Discard the herbs before serving.**

OATMEAL APPLES

1 lb Bramley apples
3 oz oatmeal
3 oz soft brown sugar
2 oz butter
cinnamon
cream

Peel, core and slice the apples. Place a layer of apple slices in an ovenware dish. Cover with a layer of oatmeal. Sprinkle with cinnamon, brown sugar and nuts of butter. Repeat these alternate layers until the ingredients are all used. **Bake in a moderate oven for 45 minutes. Serve with cream.**

CHAMPIGNONS A LA CREME

½ lb button mushrooms
1 clove garlic
2 oz butter
salt, pepper
½ tsp lemon juice
½ gill double cream
1 tsp chopped parsley

Remove the stalks of the mushrooms, using them for flavouring soups or casseroles. Place the whole mushroom caps in a thick pan, together with the crushed garlic, butter, lemon juice, salt and pepper. Cook gently, uncovered, for about 10 minutes. Spoon in the cream and stir over the heat for a few minutes. Sprinkle in the parsley, stir for a moment longer, then serve with soft rolls for dunking into the delicious sauce.

MARINADED FILLETS OF BEEF

4 fillet steaks
1 tbs oil
1 clove garlic
sprig fresh rosemary
½ gill vermouth
salt, pepper

Rub the steaks all over with crushed garlic. Put the vermouth, oil and rosemary in a dish. Season with salt and pepper. Marinade the steaks in this for at least 2 hours, turning them from time to time. Dry them well, before grilling or frying them in the usual way.

BROAD BEAN AND TOMATO SALAD

½ lb tiny new broad beans
½ orange
½ lb tomatoes
salt, pepper
6 dess olive oil
2 dess vinegar
½ tsp French mustard

Shell the beans. Peel and slice the tomatoes. Whisk together the oil, vinegar, salt, pepper, French mustard and the grated rind of ½ orange. Mix together the raw beans and tomato slices. Pour over the dressing and toss gently but thoroughly.

STRAWBERRY SORBET

1 lb strawberries
4 oz sugar
½ gill water
1 tbs lemon juice
1 tbs orange juice

Hull the strawberries, and press them through a nylon sieve, using a wooden spoon. Boil together the sugar and water for 5 minutes. Allow it to cool, then stir it into the strawberry puree. Blend in the orange juice and lemon juice. Mix well, and pour into an ice-making tray. Cover with foil, and freeze at maximum temperature for at least 2½ hours, agitating the mixture with a fork twice during the freezing period.

PIMENTO SOUP

1 large green pepper
1 onion
2 oz butter
½ oz flour
1 pint chicken stock
¾ pint milk
salt, pepper
tarragon

Finely chop the pepper and peeled onion. Heat 1 oz butter in a saucepan and toss the onion and pepper in this until soft but not brown. Add the boiling stock and a few fresh or dried tarragon leaves. Allow to simmer for 10 minutes. Liquidize this mixture, or press it through a sieve. In a second pan melt the remaining butter. Sprinkle in the flour, stir well over a gentle heat and gradually add the hot milk, stirring all the time. Allow to cook gently for 5 minutes, still stirring, then blend in the onion and pepper purée. Reheat without boiling.

DUCK WITH VERMOUTH

1–4 lb duck
1 gill vermouth
½ gill double cream
2 egg yolks
1½ oz butter
salt, pepper
1 gill duck or chicken
  stock
  stuffing of choice

Stuff the duck with your favourite stuffing. Melt the butter in a roasting tray. When hot, add the stuffed and seasoned duck, and brown it quickly all over. Pour over the stock and vermouth, cover the tin and cook in a moderate oven for 1¼ hours, basting frequently. When cooked, transfer the duck to a hot serving dish. Strain the gravy. Beat together the egg yolks and cream. Gradually add the strained sauce, stirring all the time. Reheat gently, without boiling, and check the seasoning. Serve this sauce with the duck.

GARLIC POTATOES

2 lb potatoes
2 cloves garlic
3 oz butter
1 tsp gros sel (coarse
  sea salt)

Scrub but do not peel the potatoes. Boil them in salted water until almost cooked. Drain and peel them. Cut them into irregular shapes. Place them in an ovenware dish with the butter, crushed garlic and gros sel. Cook in a moderate oven for 30 minutes, turning the potatoes from time to time.

COFFEE CREAM

1 pint milk
2 oz coffee
6 egg yolks
3 egg whites
3 tbs cream
4 oz castor sugar

Make 1 gill strong coffee, in your favourite way. Strain it into the milk. Whisk together the sugar, egg yolks and cream. Fold in the stiffly beaten egg whites. Add all this to the coffee-flavoured milk. Heat it gently in a double boiler until it thickens, stirring all the time. Pour into a serving dish and allow to cool. Sprinkle with demerara sugar just before serving.

EGGS STUFFED WITH MUSHROOMS

4 eggs
4 oz button mushrooms
1½ oz butter
salt, pepper
lemon juice
2 tbs white sauce

Hardboil the eggs, cool them, shell them under cold running water and halve them lengthwise. Scoop out and finely chop the yolks. Heat the butter in a small pan. Add the mushrooms, salt, pepper and a few drops of lemon juice. Cook gently for 8–10 minutes. Blend in the white sauce and finely chopped egg yolks. Stuff the egg whites with this mixture, place them in a buttered, ovenware dish and bake in a low oven until lightly browned.

SWEET AND SOUR MEAT BALLS

1 lb minced pork
1 clove garlic
1½ oz flour
2 oz fresh white bread-
   crumbs
salt, pepper
1 egg yolk
butter and oil for frying

for sauce:
3 oz sugar
4 tbs garlic vinegar
3 tbs soy sauce
1½ level tbs cornflour
½ pint water
1 green pepper
½ lb tomatoes
11 oz can crushed
   pineapple

Blend together the meat, garlic, ½ oz flour, breadcrumbs, salt, pepper and egg yolk. Form the mixture into small balls, roll them in the remaining flour and fry them in the hot oil and butter for 20 minutes, turning them frequently. Meanwhile, place the sugar, vinegar, and soy sauce in a pan. Blend the cornflour with a little of the water, and add this to the ingredients in the pan together with the remaining water. Bring to the boil, stirring all the time. Allow to simmer gently for 5 minutes, then add the pepper, previously cut into strips and plunged into boiling water for 2–3 minutes. Add the skinned and chopped tomatoes and pineapple. Simmer gently for 5 minutes, then pour this sauce over the meat balls before serving.

CUCUMBER SALAD WITH YOGURT

1 cucumber
1 clove garlic
1 tbs salt
1 tbs wine vinegar
1 tbs olive oil
1 tbs chopped dill or
   chives
1 carton natural yogurt

Peel and thinly slice the cucumber. Put it in a colander, sprinkle it with coarse salt, cover with a saucer then a heavy weight and allow to drain for 1 hour. Crush the garlic into the vinegar. Add the salt and mix to a smooth paste. Stir this into the yogurt. Add the oil and dill. Pour this dressing over the cucumber, toss well and sprinkle with more dill.

TANGERINE CREME BRULEE

1½ pints double cream
4 tangerines or mandarins
6 egg yolks
2 oz castor sugar
sugar for topping

Whisk together the egg yolks and castor sugar for 5 minutes. Add to the cream the grated rind of 4 tangerines and the strained juice of 2 tangerines. Heat this flavoured cream almost to boiling point, then pour it on to the egg yolks, stirring all the time. Strain this creamy custard into a double saucepan and cook gently until the mixture coats the spoon. It should be stirred constantly during this operation. Pour it into an ovenware soufflé dish and allow it to cool. Chill in the refrigerator overnight. Sprinkle the surface thickly with castor sugar and grill for a few minutes, until golden brown. Chill for a further 1 hour before serving.

6

FLAKED FISH WITH GARLIC MAYONNAISE

¾ lb white fish
2 oz prawns
½ pint mayonnaise
1 large clove garlic
2 tbs finely chopped
    parsley
1 tbs capers
lettuce

Crush the garlic and blend it into the mayonnaise, together with the parsley and capers. Choose any white fish—it need not have a very delicate flavour since the sauce is quite powerful. Steam or boil the fish quite plainly. Allow it to cool, then flake it, discarding any skin or bones. Blend it, together with the prawns, into the garlic mayonnaise. Serve on shredded lettuce.

LAMB CUTLETS WITH DUKE OF CUMBERLAND'S SAUCE

4 chump chops
salt, pepper
1 lb tomatoes
3 rashers bacon or ham
2 small onions
1 clove garlic
3 tbs vinegar
cayenne pepper

Peel and slice the tomatoes and onions. Place them in a saucepan together with the diced bacon or ham, crushed garlic, salt and pepper. Cook gently until of purée consistency. Press this sauce through a sieve and allow it to cool. Then stir in the vinegar and a pinch of cayenne pepper. Season the chops and grill them in the usual way. Meanwhile, reheat the tomato sauce, so that it is ready to pour over the cooked chops before serving.

RICE SALAD

½ lb Italian rice
½ cucumber
2 stalks celery
1 red pepper
1 small tin sweetcorn
    kernels
1 tbs sultanas
1 tbs chopped almonds
6–8 black olives
2 tbs finely chopped parsley
salt, pepper
1 clove garlic
3 tbs olive oil
½ lemon

Boil the rice in salted water for 12 minutes. Drain it and allow it to cool. Rub a salad bowl with a cut clove of garlic. Put the rice in the bowl. Add the drained contents of the tin of sweetcorn. Peel and chop the cucumber. Add this, together with the chopped celery, almonds, sultanas, stoned olives and parsley. Season with salt and pepper. Whisk together the oil and the juice of ½ lemon. Pour this over the rice and vegetables and toss well. Cut the red pepper into rings, discarding the seeds. Pour boiling water over the rings and allow to stand for 2–3 minutes, then refresh with cold water. Decorate the top of the rice salad with these red pepper rings.

ORANGE CREAM

3 oranges
3 large eggs
½ oz butter
½ pint double cream
ground ginger
2½ oz icing sugar

Strain the juice of the oranges into a small thick pan. Add the beaten eggs, a pinch of ground ginger, the cream and sifted icing sugar. Stir until well blended, then place this pan inside a larger pan of boiling water. Stir over a very low heat, until the mixture is thick and smooth. Remove the pan from the heat and plunge the small pan into a bowl of ice cubes. Add the butter, cut into tiny pieces, and continue to stir until the mixture is almost cold. Transfer to serving dishes.

ICED CUCUMBER AND YOGURT SOUP

1 cucumber
4 cupfuls yogurt
½ gill single cream
1 clove garlic
salt, pepper
1 tbs finely chopped mint

Before preparing this soup it is important to make sure that all its ingredients are well chilled. Slice the cucumber thinly, peeling it if you prefer it that way. Place it in a colander, sprinkle it with salt, and allow it to drain for 30 minutes. Beat together the cream and yogurt, until creamy. Blend in the squeezed cucumber and mint. Rub the soup tureen with the cut clove of garlic. Pour in the soup, and top with a little more finely chopped mint. Serve very cold.

COTES DE VEAU EN CASSEROLE

4 veal cutlets
2 large onions
2 oz butter
1 wineglassful sherry
   or vermouth
salt, pepper
3 oz fresh brown
   breadcrumbs
1 gill beef or chicken
   stock

Peel and chop the onions. Fry them in the butter until golden, then add the sherry or vermouth. Allow to simmer for 2–3 minutes. Season the cutlets with salt and pepper, then roll them in the breadcrumbs, to coat them thickly. Butter an ovenware dish and put a layer of breadcrumbs in the bottom. Arrange the cutlets on top of this, then pour the onion mixture over the top. Cook without a lid in a very low oven for about 1 hour, adding a little stock from time to time, as necessary.

CURRIED CABBAGE

1 small cabbage
1 dess curry powder
2 tbs tomato ketchup
salt, pepper
1 clove garlic
1 large onion
2 tbs mango chutney
2 tbs oil

Heat the oil in a large, thick pan. Add the crushed garlic and peeled, sliced onion. Stir in the curry powder and allow to cook for 8–10 minutes, stirring from time to time. Add the finely shredded cabbage, chutney, ketchup, salt and pepper. Stir well, and cook for a further 8–10 minutes, adding a few drops of stock or water if the mixture becomes too dry.

RHUBARB TANSY

1 lb rhubarb
4 oz butter
3 oz sugar
2 egg yolks
1 gill cream
1 lemon
1½ oz castor sugar

Heat the butter. Cut the cleaned rhubarb into 1 inch lengths. Cook them in the butter (together with a little water if necessary) until tender. Remove from the heat. Add the egg yolks and cream, previously lightly beaten together. Blend in the sugar. Taste for sweetness. Reheat gently, without allowing to boil. Transfer the tansy to a serving dish. Sprinkle it with castor sugar and the juice of 1 lemon.

8

DANISH SHRIMPS

8 slices brown or rye
  bread
2 oz butter
½ lb peeled shrimps
salt, pepper
½ lemon

The Danes, who have the most tender, most succulent shrimps in the world, do not drown them in mayonnaise. They simply pile them, in mini-pyramids, on thickly buttered slices of rye or brown bread. Then they sprinkle them with a little salt, masses of freshly ground black pepper and a trickle of fresh lemon juice. Check the flavour of your shrimps before serving them in the Danish style. They may need no salt, or they may not be quite super enough to stand up to this fairly severe flavour test.

KIDNEY AND ONION CASSEROLE

4 pig's or 12 lamb's
  kidneys
salt, pepper
1 large onion
flour
¾ pint beef stock
parsley
marjoram

Cut the kidneys into smallish pieces, discarding the fat from the centres. Toss them in flour and arrange them in an ovenware casserole dish, together with the peeled and sliced onion. Season with salt, pepper and large pinches of finely chopped parsley and marjoram. Barely cover with stock and cook, covered, in a low oven for 2 hours.

POTATO AND TOMATO SALAD

1½ lb new potatoes
3 large tomatoes
1 small onion
½ pint mayonnaise
1 tbs single cream
salt, pepper

Boil the potatoes in salted water, without peeling them. When cooked, allow them to cool, then peel them and cut them into slices. Blend in the peeled, sliced tomatoes and the peeled, finely chopped onion. Season with salt and pepper. Mix together the mayonnaise and cream. Pour this over the potatoes and tomatoes and mix thoroughly, but gently.

POIRES SAVOIE

2 lb ripe conference pears
½ oz butter
5 oz castor sugar
1 gill double cream
vanilla pod

Peel, core and quarter the pears. Heat the butter in a large frying pan. Arrange the pears in this, in a single layer if possible. Sprinkle them with the sugar and add a small piece of vanilla pod. Cover and allow to simmer gently until the pears are soft. Pour over the cream and cook for a further few minutes until the cream thickens. Transfer to a moderate oven until golden skin forms on the surface, and serve hot.

9

BRETON SOUP

1 lb haricot beans
2 large onions
1 lb tomatoes
2 carrots
1 bay leaf
sprig of parsley
sprig of thyme
salt, pepper
1¾ pints chicken stock
   or water
1½ oz butter

Soak the beans in cold water for 8 hours. Drain and rinse them. Put them in a large pan together with the parsley, thyme and bay leaf. Add the stock or water, bring to the boil and allow to simmer until the beans are very tender. Meanwhile, heat the butter in a second pan. Add the peeled and chopped carrots and onions, and fry until golden brown. Add the peeled and roughly chopped tomatoes and allow to cook gently for 20 minutes. Add this mixture to the beans, season to taste, allow to cook together for 10 minutes, then liquidize, or press the mixture through a sieve.

JUGGED NECK OF LAMB

2 lb best end neck of
   lamb
1½ oz butter
4 small tomatoes
1 stick celery
salt, pepper
½ pint stock
1 tbs plain flour
1 tbs lemon juice
2 tbs redcurrant jelly
1 tbs chopped parsley
½ gill port or sherry
2 onions

Peel and quarter the onions. Toss them in ½ oz butter over a moderate heat until lightly browned. Cut the lamb into chops, trimming off fat. Brown the chops in the pan with the onions. Peel the tomatoes and slice them. Chop the celery. Arrange the tomatoes and celery in the bottom of a greased casserole dish. Add the chops and onions. Season with salt and pepper. Heat 1 oz butter in a pan. Add the flour, stir well and allow to cook until lightly browned. Gradually stir in the stock and lemon juice. Mix well and pour this sauce over the chops. Cover with a lid and bake in a moderate oven for 2 hours. Ten minutes before serving stir the redcurrant jelly, parsley and port into the sauce.

PETITS POIS A LA FRANCAISE

1 lb very young peas
1 lettuce
6 spring onions
1½ oz butter
1 tsp sugar
salt
thyme

Melt the butter in a thick pan. Add the chopped onions and shredded lettuce and allow to cook gently for 5 minutes. Add the shelled peas, sugar, salt and a sprig of thyme. Cover the pan with a soup plate filled with water, to prevent drying, and cook gently until the peas are tender.

LEMON CURD TARTLETS

½ lb short sweet pastry
3 oz butter
3 large eggs
6 oz castor sugar
2 lemons

Line individual tartlet cases with short pastry and bake them blind. Allow them to cool. Put the butter, sugar, finely grated rind and strained juice of 2 lemons in a small thick pan. Place this in a larger pan of boiling water. Blend together well, and when the butter has melted add the well beaten eggs. Continue to stir, over the heat, until the mixture thickens. This will take about 10 minutes. Remove from the heat and allow to cool, stirring from time to time. When quite cold, fill each tartlet with this lemon curd, and decorate with some flaked chocolate or a maraschino cherry.

TOMATO, MUSHROOM AND OLIVE SALAD

6 large tomatoes
4 oz button mushrooms
1 small onion
8–10 black olives
6 tbs olive oil
2 tbs wine vinegar
½ tsp French mustard
salt, pepper
pinch ground cinnamon

Wipe the mushrooms and slice them. Place them in a plastic container with an airtight lid. Add the olives and finely sliced onion. Whisk together the oil, vinegar, salt pepper, mustard and cinnamon. Pour this over the mushrooms, cover with the lid and allow to marinade for 1 hour, turning it over from time to time. Peel and slice the tomatoes. Add them to the mushrooms and toss well before serving with slices of crusty French bread and butter.

VEAL FRICASSEE

2 lb lean veal
2 oz butter
2 oz flour
1 pint water or chicken
   stock
salt, pepper
1 bay leaf
sprig thyme
parsley
1 celery stalk
½ lb tiny onions
½ lb button mushrooms
1 gill single cream
½ lemon
cayenne pepper

Cut the veal into neat squares. Heat the butter in a thick pan, add the veal and sauté it for a few minutes, without allowing it to brown. Sprinkle in the flour, stir well and gradually add the boiling water or stock, stirring all the time. Season with salt and pepper, and add the bay leaf, thyme, parsley and celery stalk, all tied together. Cover the pan and allow to cook gently for 1½ hours. When almost cooked, blend in the hot cream. Season with a pinch of cayenne pepper, and the juice of ½ lemon. Separately boil the onions and mushrooms until cooked. Blend them into the fricassée, and reheat gently before serving.

POMMES DE TERRE PROVENCALES

2 lb potatoes
5 tbs olive oil
3 large onions
2 cloves garlic
nutmeg
½ lemon
salt, pepper

Put the oil in a thick pan. On top of this put the chopped onions and garlic, mixed together. On top of this place the potatoes, peeled and halved if new; cut into pieces if old. Add salt, pepper, a pinch of freshly grated nutmeg and a small piece of lemon peel. Cover the pan with a tight-fitting lid and cook over a low heat for 15 minutes, during which time the pan must not be moved, nor its contents stirred. After 15 minutes, stir the contents, to mix the potatoes with the onions and garlic, and cook for a further 30 minutes, or until the potatoes are cooked. Then remove the lid and allow to cook quickly for a few minutes, to reduce the liquid. Transfer the potatoes to a hot serving dish. Add the juice of ½ lemon to the juices left in the pan, heat for 2 minutes, then pour this over the potatoes before serving.

PINEAPPLE CREME BRULEE

1 fresh pineapple
1 tbs castor sugar
2 tbs kirsch or brandy
½ pint double cream
4 oz demerara sugar

Cut the pineapple into cubes, discarding any tough pieces. Arrange them in an ovenware soufflé dish, sprinkle them with the castor sugar and kirsch. Whip the cream until thick. Cover the pineapple with the cream and allow to stand in the refrigerator overnight. Spread the demerara sugar over the top, and pop under the grill for a few minutes, until the sugar caramelizes. Serve at once.

PETITS POIS SOUP

5–6 oz petits pois (tinned or frozen would do)
1 oz boiled ham
1 small onion
1½ pints chicken stock
1 lemon
2 eggs
½ gill single cream
salt, pepper
sugar
1 oz butter
mint

Melt the butter in a thick pan. Add the finely chopped onion and allow to cook gently until soft but not brown. Add the ham, cut into strips, then add the peas. Stir well, season with salt, pepper, a pinch of sugar and a sprig of mint. Barely cover with boiling water and simmer gently until the peas are tender. Stir in the cream. Beat together the eggs and the juice of 1 lemon. Stir this into the hot, but not boiling soup, away from the heat. Also add the hot, but not boiling stock, stirring all the time to prevent curdling. Serve at once.

WINE BAKED PORK

1½ lb pork fillet
3 oz butter
1 tbs flour
1½ cupfuls milk
2 tbs sliced green pepper
½ gill white wine or vermouth

Trim the meat of any sinews or fat. Cut the meat into 1 inch cubes. Heat the butter in a thick frying pan. Add the meat and cook it with the lid on for 20 minutes, over a moderate heat. Remove the lid, increase the heat slightly, and cook until the meat is light brown all over. Add the flour and stir it in well, then gradually blend in the warm milk and stir until the sauce is smooth. Add the green pepper, salt and pepper. Transfer the mixture to a greased casserole dish and bake in a moderate oven for 45 minutes. When the meat is almost cooked, stir in the wine, then continue to cook until the meat is quite tender.

GRATIN D'OIGNONS

2 lb onions
½ pint basic white sauce
salt, pepper
2 oz brown breadcrumbs
1 tbs oil
2 tbs finely chopped parsley

Peel and slice the onions. Boil them in salted water until almost tender. Drain them well. Mix them with the hot white sauce and place in an ovenware dish. Season well with salt and pepper. Sprinkle with the breadcrumbs and parsley, previously blended together. Sprinkle with the oil and cook in a moderate oven until crisp and brown on top.

CHOCOLATE AND ALMOND CAKE

3 oz unsalted butter
3 oz castor sugar
4 oz bitter chocolate
3 oz ground almonds
3 eggs
1 tbs strong black coffee
1 tbs whisky

This is more like a rich, moist pudding than a conventional cake, but ideal as a cadenza to a fine meal. It has no flour, so do not expect it to rise to giddy heights. Break up the chocolate. Put it in a shallow ovenware dish together with the coffee and whisky, in a low oven until the chocolate has melted. Transfer this mixture to a pan. Add the butter, sugar and ground almonds, and stir over a gentle heat until the mixture is well blended. Remove from the heat. Separate the eggs. Add the egg yolks, one at a time, to the chocolate mixture, beating well between each addition. Stiffly whisk the egg whites, and fold them into the mixture. Transfer to a lightly buttered sandwich tin. Stand it on a baking sheet and bake in a very low oven, Reg. 1, for 45 minutes. Remove the ring section of the sandwich tin, but leave the cake standing on the base for serving. It is very fragile, and might well crack if transferred to a different plate.

CELERY SOUP

2 heads celery
3 oz lean bacon
2 oz butter
2 oz flour
1½ pints chicken stock
2 tbs double cream
salt, pepper

Dice the celery and bacon. Heat the butter in a thick pan, and add the celery and bacon. Toss it well over a low flame until it begins to colour. Sprinkle in the flour, and gradually add the boiling stock, stirring all the time. Allow to simmer for 15–20 minutes. Liquidize, or rub the mixture through a sieve. Check the seasoning. Reheat and stir in the cream before serving. It is wise to season this soup at the end of cooking, because the bacon contributes quite a strong flavour to the soup and might make further seasoning unnecessary.

SPRING LAMB

1 joint spring lamb
salt, pepper
tarragon
2 cloves garlic
1 cupful fresh brown
  breadcrumbs
½ cupful finely chopped
  parsley
1 oz butter

Make a few small incisions in the lamb joint, and insert a small sliver of garlic in each. Season the meat with salt and pepper, and roast it in the usual way, with a sprig of tarragon. Ten minutes before the meat is ready for serving remove it from the oven, coat it with the breadcrumbs and parsley, previously blended together and seasoned with freshly milled black pepper. Pour over the melted butter and return to a hot oven for a further 10 minutes, after which time the topping should be brown and crisp.

DANISH RED CABBAGE

1 red cabbage
1 medium onion
1 oz butter
salt, pepper
cayenne pepper
nutmeg
1 dess castor sugar
1 tbs vinegar

Slice the cabbage finely. Cover it with cold water and allow to soak for 30 minutes, then drain it well. Place it in a pan, together with the butter, finely chopped onion, ½ tsp salt, ½ tsp cayenne pepper and ½ tsp finely grated nutmeg. Cover with a lid and allow to cook gently for 1 hour, adding a little water if necessary. Add the sugar and vinegar and continue to cook for a further 5 minutes before serving.

STRAWBERRY ICE CREAM

1 lb strawberries
4 oz sugar
½ gill water
1 tbs orange juice
1 tbs lemon juice
½ gill double cream

Hull the strawberries, and press them through a nylon sieve with a wooden spoon. Boil together the sugar and water for 5 minutes. Allow this to cool, then stir it into the fruit purée. Add the lemon and orange juice. Fold in the whipped cream thoroughly, so that no traces of white remain. Pour into an ice-making tray, cover with foil and freeze at the maximum temperature for 2½–3 hours, agitating the mixture with a fork twice during the freezing period.

SHRIMPS WITH GREEN MAYONNAISE

6 oz peeled shrimps
2 eggs
1½ oz watercress
1½ oz spinach
1 tbs finely chopped
  parsley
1 tbs finely chopped
  chives
1 tbs finely chopped
  tarragon
½ pint mayonnaise

Hardboil the eggs. Shell and quarter them. Plunge the watercress, spinach, parsley, chives and tarragon into boiling water for 2 minutes, then rinse them in cold water and drain well. Pound them to a paste in a mortar, or liquidize them together with a little of the mayonnaise. Blend in the remaining mayonnaise. Arrange the egg quarters round the edge of a serving plate. Pile the shrimps in the middle and coat with the green mayonnaise.

MEAT LOAF COOKED IN TOMATO SAUCE

1½ lb minced lean pork
1 slice bread
1 gill milk
1 small onion
1 tbs chopped parsley
½ tsp sage
salt, pepper
3 eggs
flour
2 oz butter
4 tomatoes
4 tbs sherry

Toast the bread, then soak it in the milk. Stir it into the minced pork, together with the finely sliced onion, parsley, sage, salt and pepper. Bind the mixture with one of the eggs. Hardboil the other two eggs. Using floured hands, shape the pork mixture into two oblongs, of equal size. Shell and slice the hardboiled eggs. Arrange them along the middle of one of the meat oblongs, cover with the second oblong, and place this meat loaf sandwich in a roasting tray, together with the butter. Bake in a moderate oven for 45 minutes. Peel the tomatoes and rub them through a sieve. Add this tomato purée to the meat loaf and cook for a further 40 minutes.

SWEET AND SOUR ONIONS

1 lb onions
1 gill garlic vinegar
2 tbs oil
2 tbs castor sugar
salt, pepper

Peel and slice the onions. Heat the oil in a thick pan, add the onions and allow to cook gently until golden brown. Blend in the vinegar, sugar, salt and pepper. Allow to simmer gently for 30 minutes.

PEAR CRUMBLE

1½ lb pears
2 oz crystallized ginger
2 oz sugar

for crumble:
4 oz butter
4 oz castor sugar
4 oz flour
2 oz ground almonds

Peel, core and slice the pears. Arrange them, with the chopped ginger, in the bottom of an ovenware dish. Sprinkle with the sugar. Rub together the flour, butter, sugar and ground almonds until of a crumb consistency. Cover the fruit with this mixture. Bake in a moderate oven for 1½ hours, covering with a lid or buttered paper for the first hour.

LETTUCE AND EGG GRATIN

½ lb lettuce
1 oz butter
salt, pepper
sugar
4 eggs
1 gill single cream

for sauce:
1 oz butter
1 tbs flour
½ pint milk

Melt the butter in a thick pan, add the shredded lettuce leaves, cover with a lid and allow to cook gently for 10 minutes. Then season with salt, pepper and a pinch of sugar. Make a basic white sauce with 1 oz butter, 1 tbs flour and ½ pint milk. Add the cooked lettuce. Hardboil the eggs, shell them under cold running water, and quarter them. Blend them gently into the lettuce sauce. Stir in the cream. Pour the mixture into an oven-ware dish, cover with the breadcrumbs and dot with nuts of butter. Bake in a moderate oven for 10 minutes.

PORK CHOPS WITH PINEAPPLE

4 pork chops
flour
salt, pepper
½ pint pineapple juice
4 pineapple rings
1 bay leaf
sprig of thyme
2 cloves
1 clove garlic
2 stalks celery
1 tsp arrowroot
2 oz butter

Dust the pork chops with seasoned flour. Heat the butter in a frying pan, and sear the chops on both sides in this. Transfer them to a casserole dish. Season with salt and pepper, and pour in the pineapple juice. Fry the pineapple rings on both sides in the butter, then add them to the chops, together with the bay leaf, chopped celery, cloves, thyme and crushed garlic. Bake in a moderate oven for 1½ hours. Transfer the chops to a serving plate, and keep them warm. Meanwhile, strain the juice into a pan. Blend the arrowroot with 2 tbs water. Add this to the juice. Reheat, stirring well, and pour this over the chops before serving.

CAULIFLOWER SALAD

1 cauliflower
salt, pepper
3 tbs oil
1 tbs vinegar
1 tsp French mustard

Finely grate the raw cauliflower, using only the white part. Whisk together the oil, vinegar, salt, pepper and mustard. Blend this into the grated cauliflower, mix well and serve cold. As this salad looks rather more like elderly porridge than anything else, it looks better in a coloured dish, or in a white dish lined with lettuce leaves. Top it with a few black olives or tomato slices for extra colour.

COLD LEMON SOUFFLE

4 lemons
4 eggs
salt
6 oz castor sugar
½ oz gelatine
½ pint double cream
1 tsp kirsch or other liqueur

Separate the eggs. Beat together the egg yolks, sugar and a pinch of salt for 10 minutes. Add the finely grated rind and strained juice of 4 lemons. Beat for a further 5 minutes, then add the kirsch or other liqueur. Melt the gelatine in 2 tbs of very hot water, until completely dissolved. Whisk the egg whites until stiff. Add the gelatine to the lemon mixture, stir well, then gently fold in the beaten egg whites. Make sure that no traces of white remain, and transfer the mixture to a serving bowl. Chill. To give a splash of colour, garnish the soufflé with a few fresh raspberries or a spray of cherries.

THON GRATINEE

1 medium tin tuna fish
4 tomatoes
1 gill stock
1 gill single cream
salt, pepper
2 oz butter
1 oz flour
3 oz fresh breadcrumbs

Heat 1 oz butter in a saucepan. Sprinkle in the flour, stir well, then gradually add the stock, stirring all the time. Gradually add the cream, still stirring. Season with pepper and just a little salt. Drain the tuna fish, and flake it with a fork. Blend it into the sauce and reheat gently, without allowing it to bubble. Pour the mixture into an ovenware dish. Cover with the breadcrumbs, dot with the remaining butter and grill until brown. Meanwhile, peel, slice and lightly fry the tomatoes. Top the breadcrumbs with the tomato slices before serving.

KIDNEYS IN WINE SAUCE

6 lamb's kidneys
4 oz button mushrooms
3½ oz butter
1 tbs flour
1 gill red wine
4 tbs stock
1 clove garlic
thyme
1 bay leaf
salt, pepper
½ lemon

Melt 1 oz butter in a thick pan. Sprinkle in the flour and stir over a gentle flame for a few minutes, until golden brown. Gradually add the wine and stock, crushed garlic, a sprig of thyme, bay leaf, salt and pepper. Stir well and allow to simmer gently for 15 minutes. Skin, core and quarter the kidneys. Sprinkle them with the juice of ½ lemon. Heat the remaining butter in a pan. Fry the kidneys and sliced mushrooms in this for 10 minutes. Strain the wine sauce into a clean saucepan. Blend in the kidneys and mushrooms, and reheat gently, without allowing to boil.

SPROUTS WITH ONIONS

1½ lb sprouts
salt, pepper
2 large onions
1 oz butter
1 dess paprika
2 oz fresh white bread-
    crumbs

Wash the sprouts carefully, discarding any damaged leaves. Allow them to soak in lukewarm salted water for 10 minutes. Boil in salted water for 10 minutes. Heat the butter in a second pan. Add the peeled, chopped onions and fry until soft and golden. Add the drained sprouts, paprika and breadcrumbs and cook for 5 minutes, stirring all the time.

RHUBARB FOOL

1 lb rhubarb
2–3 oz demerara sugar
½ pint double cream

Cut the rhubarb into 1 inch lengths and put it in a saucepan, together with the sugar and 1 gill water. Bring to the boil and allow to simmer until the rhubarb is tender enough to be rubbed through a sieve. Check for sweetness, then allow to cool. When quite cold fold in the whipped cream.

BAKED GRAPEFRUIT

2 large grapefruit
4 tsp soft brown sugar
4 tsp brandy or rum
4 sprigs mint

Halve the grapefruit. Using a grapefruit knife, loosen all the segments. Sprinkle each grapefruit half with soft brown sugar, then brandy or rum, and allow to stand for 1 hour. Just before serving, pop them under the grill for a few moments, to lightly brown. Top each with a sprig of mint before serving.

PORK MEAT BALLS WITH TOMATO SAUCE

1 lb minced lean pork
1 egg
salt, pepper
1 medium onion
parsley
fresh tarragon or basil
3 oz butter
1 gill boiling water
1 tbs tomato purée

Blend together the meat, beaten egg, salt, pepper and 1 tbs finely chopped tarragon or basil. Grate the peeled onion, and parboil it in salted water for 5 minutes. Drain it well, then blend it into the pork. Finely chop a large bunch of parsley. With wet hands form the meat mixture into small balls and roll them in the chopped parsley until well covered. Heat the butter in a frying pan. Toss the meat balls in this until seared all over. Dilute the tomato purée in the boiling water. Pour this over the meat balls and allow to simmer until cooked, about 20 minutes.

COURGETTES IN CREAM

1½ lb courgettes
salt, pepper
3 oz butter
½ gill double cream
dill

Cut the courgettes into slices. Parboil them in salted water for 5 minutes, then drain well. Heat the butter in a pan. Add the drained courgettes and toss them over the heat for 5–10 minutes, or until tender. Season with salt and pepper. Pour over the cream, stir well, and when thoroughly heated, transfer the courgettes and cream to a serving dish. Serve sprinkled with finely chopped fresh, or dried, dill.

ALMOND CREAM

½ pint double cream
2 egg whites
2 oz sugar
pinch of salt
4 oz flaked almonds
2 tsp vermouth

Whip the cream until it is thick but not too stiff. Whisk the egg whites stiffly. Fold the sugar and salt gently into the egg whites. Pop the almonds under the grill until lightly toasted. Fold all but 2 tbs of them into them into the egg whites. Blend in the cream and vermouth. Transfer to a serving dish, sprinkle with the remaining almonds and chill before serving.

SPROUT SOUP

2 lbs sprouts
½ oz flour
2 pints chicken stock
2 oz butter
salt, pepper
½ gill cream

Wash the sprouts, and boil them in salted water until quite tender. Drain them well. Melt the butter in a thick pan. Add the drained sprouts. Sprinkle with the flour, and stir well. Gradually add the boiling stock. Cook quickly until the sprouts are very soft, seasoning with salt and pepper. Liquidize or rub the mixture through a sieve. Blend in the cream before serving.

GIGOT D'AGNEAU A LA FERMIERE

3 lb leg of lamb
1 gill sherry
1 gill stock
½ lb turnips
½ lb carrots
1½ lb fresh peas
12 new potatoes
1 gill cream
2 oz butter
salt, pepper
sugar
½ oz flour

Melt the butter in a large, thick pan. Toss the meat in this until golden all over. Pour over the sherry and allow to bubble for a few minutes. Add the stock. Cover the pan and allow to cook in a moderate oven for 30 minutes. Add the peeled carrots, turnips and potatoes—whole if small enough; otherwise halved. Cook for a further 10 minutes, then add the shelled peas. Season with salt, pepper and a pinch of sugar. Cook gently for a further hour, or until the meat and vegetables are quite tender. Transfer the lamb and vegetables to a serving dish and keep them warm. Pour off any excess fat from the sauce. Sprinkle in ½ oz flour, stir well, and add the boiling cream. Allow this sauce to cook for a further 10 minutes, before pouring it over the meat and vegetables.

AVOCADO AND TOMATO SALAD

2 small avocados
½ lb tomatoes
salt, pepper
3 spring onions
6 tbs olive oil
2 tbs vinegar
½ tsp French mustard

Peel and slice the tomatoes. Peel and slice the avocados, discarding the stones. Whisk together the salt, pepper, oil, vinegar and mustard. Blend together, gently but thoroughly, the avocado, tomato, finely chopped spring onions and dressing.

APRICOT ICE CREAM

1 lb apricots
3 oz sugar
1 gill double cream

Halve and stone the apricots. Steam them until soft, then liquidize them. Allow to cool. Simmer together the sugar and 1 gill water for 10 minutes, to produce a syrup. Allow it to cool, then stir it into the apricot purée. Fold in the whipped cream. Pour the mixture into an ice-making tray, cover with foil and allow to freeze at maximum temperature for 2½–3 hours, agitating the mixture with a fork twice during the freezing period.

TERRINE OF LIVER

1 lb pig's or ox liver
3 cloves garlic
10 rashers bacon
salt, pepper
rosemary
¼ glassful whisky

Mince the liver coarsely. Blend in the crushed garlic, 3 finely diced bacon rashers, salt, pepper and some finely chopped fresh rosemary. Line an ovenware terrine dish with bacon. Fill it with the liver mixture. Pour over the whisky. Cover with more bacon rashers, then the lid. Cook in a moderate oven for 1 hour. Remove the lid, cover the top with greaseproof paper, and put a weight on top, to press it while it cools. Serve with hot toast, or crusty French bread.

RAGOUT DE VEAU A LA NICOISE

2 lb diced veal
1 lb tomatoes
2 large onions
salt, pepper
thyme
1 bay leaf
1 clove
12 small potatoes
15 black olives
2 oz butter
¾ pint chicken stock

Heat the butter in a thick pan. Add the diced veal, and toss it quickly over a high flame for a few minutes, until each piece of veal is brown all over. Add 1 finely chopped onion and continue to cook until the onion is soft and golden. Add the skinned, chopped tomatoes. Cover level with stock. Season with salt, pepper, a sprig of thyme, a bay leaf and 1 onion, studded with a clove. Allow to simmer gently for 45 minutes. Add the peeled potatoes, whole if small; halved if large. Add the olives. Cook gently until the potatoes are soft.

CAULIFLOWER AND CARROT SALAD

1 cauliflower
3 carrots
1 clove garlic
5 tbs olive oil
1 lemon
salt, pepper
1 tsp mustard
chives

Break up the cauliflower into sprigs. Plunge them into boiling salted water for 2 minutes, then drain them and allow to cool. Rub a salad bowl with the cut clove of garlic. Put the cauliflower and finely chopped carrots in the bowl. Mix together the oil, juice of 1 lemon, salt, pepper and mustard. Pour this over the vegetables, toss well and serve at once, sprinkled with finely chopped chives.

COMPOTE

4 oz sugar
¼ pint water
1 lemon
1 orange
1 cooking apple
4 oz blackberries
4 oz damsons
4 oz plums
4 oz golden plums

Place the sugar and water in a large thick pan. Add 2–3 large pieces of lemon rind and the strained juice of the lemon and orange. Bring to the boil, stirring until the sugar has melted. Add the peeled, cored and sliced apple and all the other fruit, whole. Allow to simmer gently until the fruit is cooked. Allow to cool, remove the pieces of lemon peel and serve with pouring cream. The fruit may be varied, according to season, but the cooking principle remains the same.

SOUPE AU PISTOU

1½ tbs olive oil
1 onion
2 tomatoes
1¾ pints water
salt, pepper
½ lb French beans
4 oz haricot beans
1 courgette
2–3 potatoes
1 leek
2 oz spaghetti

for paste:
2 cloves garlic
10 sprigs basil
3 tbs olive oil

Heat the oil in a large, thick pan. Add the peeled and sliced onion and allow to cook gently until golden. Add the skinned and chopped tomatoes and cook for a few minutes, then add the water. Season with salt and pepper and bring to the boil. Add the French beans, cut into 1 inch lengths, and the haricot beans, previously soaked and parboiled. Add the diced, unpeeled courgette, peeled and diced potatoes and chopped leek. Allow to cook gently for 10 minutes, then add the spaghetti, cut into short lengths. Allow to cook until the spaghetti is cooked. Meanwhile prepare the 'pistou'. Pound together the garlic and basil. Gradually add the oil, drop by drop. When the spaghetti is cooked and the soup ready, remove the pan from the heat and stir in the 'pistou'. Serve at once.

FILLET OF BEEF EN PAPILLOTE

4 fillet steaks
4 slices lean boiled ham
2 oz butter
4 oz mushrooms
1 medium onion
salt, pepper
oil
1 tbs whisky

Brush the trimmed fillets with whisky. Place a slice of ham on top of each fillet. Heat the butter in a frying pan. Toss the sliced mushrooms and onions in this until cooked and golden. Season them with salt and pepper. Place a spoonful of this mixture on each steak. Oil 4 pieces of foil. Place one fillet on each and wrap them securely. Cook in a hot oven for 20 minutes.

MUSHROOMS AND TOMATOES

¾ lb button mushrooms
1 large onion
4 large tomatoes
salt, pepper
2 oz butter
1 tbs oil
2 tbs finely chopped
   parsley

Heat the butter and oil together in a thick pan. Add the peeled, sliced onion and allow to cook gently until soft and golden. Add the sliced mushrooms and allow to cook for a further 5 minutes. Add the peeled, chopped tomatoes, salt, pepper and parsley. Stir well, cover the pan and allow to simmer gently for 5–10 minutes. Serve either hot or cold.

STUFFED PINEAPPLE

2 medium pineapples
4 tbs raisins
2 tbs rum
3 oz crystallized ginger
1 oz castor sugar
½ pint whipped cream

Halve the pineapples lengthwise and scoop out the flesh. Dice it. Add the raisins and rum and allow to stand for 30 minutes. Blend in the whipped cream, chopped ginger and sugar, and pile this mixture into the empty pineapple halves. Cover well and chill thoroughly before serving.

THON A LA MIROSMENIL

½ lb fresh or tinned tuna
  fish
2 tbs double cream
2 tbs mayonnaise
salt, pepper
cayenne pepper
½ lemon

Mince the tuna fish, or cream it in a liquidizer. Blend in the cream, mayonnaise, salt, pepper, a pinch of cayenne pepper and lemon juice to taste. When well blended, chill the mixture before serving with black bread or fingers of hot toast.

LAMB ROASTED WITH CORIANDER SEEDS

1 small leg of lamb
2 cloves garlic
1 tbs coriander seeds
salt, pepper
1 lb potatoes

Crush together the peeled garlic and coriander seeds. Make a few incisions in the lamb, with the point of a sharp knife. Press the crushed coriander and garlic into each incision. Rub the lamb all over with salt and pepper and roast it in the usual way. Half an hour before the meat is ready, surround it with the potatoes, previously peeled and parboiled.

GRATIN DE CELERI

2 heads celery
1 onion
2 oz butter
1 oz flour
1 pint milk
2 oz fresh white bread-
  crumbs

Scrub the celery and cut the stalks into 1-inch lengths. Boil them in salted water until almost tender, then drain well: Heat 1 oz butter in a thick pan. Add the peeled, sliced onion and allow to cook gently until soft but not brown. Sprinkle in the flour. Stir well, then gradually add the milk, stirring all the time. Allow this onion sauce to simmer for 15–20 minutes, stirring it from time to time. Arrange the celery in an ovenware dish. Pour over the onion sauce. Sprinkle with the breadcrumbs and dot with the remaining butter, cut into small pieces. Cook in a moderate oven until crisp and lightly browned.

BANANA CREAM

7–8 ripe bananas
½ pint double cream
3 tbs strawberry jam
½ lemon
2 oz castor sugar
almonds

Mash the bananas with a fork until of a smooth purée consistency. Whip the cream until stiff, and fold in the sugar. Stir in the lemon juice and strawberry jam into the banana purée. Fold in the sweetened cream and chill before serving topped with flaked, toasted almonds.

CHAMPIGNONS A LA GRECQUE

3 tbs oil
3 tbs water
2 tomatoes
6 coriander seeds
1 bay leaf
salt, pepper
sprig thyme
½ lemon
½ lb button mushrooms

In a saucepan put the oil, water, skinned and chopped tomatoes, coriander seeds, bay leaf, sprig of thyme, salt and pepper. Bring to the boil and allow to simmer for 2–3 minutes. Rub the mushrooms with lemon juice and add them to the pan. Cook gently for 5 minutes. Transfer the mushrooms to a serving dish. Cook the sauce quickly, over a high flame, until it begins to thicken. Pour it over the mushrooms and allow to cool before serving.

ROAST PORK WITH APPLES AND SULTANAS

3½ lb joint of roasting
  pork
6 medium eating apples
salt, pepper
½ pint water
4 oz mixed currants
  and sultanas
sage

Make a small incision in the skin of the pork, and insert the sprig of sage. Rub the joint with salt and pepper, and place it in a baking tin, together with the water. Bake in a moderate oven, allowing 30 minutes per 1 lb. Core but do not peel the apples. Fill the centres with mixed currants and sultanas. Surround the pork joint with these stuffed apples an hour before cooking is complete.

NORMANDY LENTILS

1 lb lentils
1 large onion
2 rashers bacon
salt, pepper
1 carrot
1 bay leaf
1 clove garlic

Allow the lentils to soak for at least 4 hours in cold water. Drain and rinse them well. Place them in a saucepan. Add the peeled carrot, peeled and sliced onion, diced bacon, bay leaf and crushed garlic. Cover level with cold water. Bring to the boil, then transfer to a fairly low oven and cook for 2½–3 hours, or until the lentils are soft. Season to taste with salt, pepper and, if liked, a teaspoonful of mustard before serving.

ALMOND WHIP

2 oz ground almonds
½ pint double cream
½ gill vermouth
1½ oz castor sugar
1 orange
2 tbs rosewater
sprig fresh rosemary
nutmeg

Whisk together the cream, ground almonds and rosewater. Stir in the vermouth and allow to stand for 20 minutes, then strain the cream through a sieve. Blend in the grated rind of 1 orange, a pinch of grated nutmeg and the rosemary, cut into tiny pieces. Stir well, then allow to stand in a cool place for 2–3 hours. Add the castor sugar. Whip the mixture until frothy. Pour it into individual serving glasses and chill before serving.

BEAN SOUP

½ lb dried haricot beans
2 pints water
6 tbs olive oil
2 large cloves
garlic
large bunch parsley
salt, pepper

Soak the beans in 2 pints of cold water, for 2–3 hours unless they are very old stock, in which case they will need overnight soaking. Cook the beans gently in the same water, without salt, until tender. Remove half of the cooked beans and sieve or liquidize them. Return them to the remaining beans and liquid. In a second pan cook the finely chopped garlic in 2 tbs of olive oil. When the garlic is cooked and golden blend it into the hot soup, together with the remaining oil, salt and masses of finely chopped parsley.

ESCALOPES DE VEAU EN PAPILLOTES

4 veal escalopes
½ lemon
salt, pepper
4 slices lean boiled ham
½ lb mushrooms
2 onions
parsley
2 oz butter

The escalopes should be well flattened. Season them with salt, pepper and lemon juice, and fry them quickly on both sides in the butter, previously heated in a thick frying pan. Cut out 4 large, heart-shaped pieces of grease-proof paper. Butter half of each heart and place a seared escalope on each buttered piece. Peel and chop the onions finely, and fry them, together with the finely sliced mushrooms, in the butter which was used for cooking the meat. When lightly cooked, blend in plenty of freshly chopped parsley. Spread some of this mixture on top of each escalope. Cover with a slice of boiled ham. Fold over the unbuttered half of paper, turning in all the edges to prevent the precious juices from escaping. Place them on a baking tray and cook in a slow oven for 20–25 minutes.

CELERIAC SALAD

2 medium celeriacs
½ pint mayonnaise
chives

Boil the celeriacs in salted water for 15–20 minutes, without peeling them. Drain them well and peel them while still hot. Slice them finely. Arrange them in a serving dish and allow to cool. Coat with mayonnaise and sprinkle with finely chopped chives before serving.

RASPBERRY CREAM

1 lb raspberries
2 egg whites
½ pint double cream
2 oz castor sugar

Whip the egg whites stiffly. Add the cream and whip again until of a mousse consistency. Sieve the raspberries, reserving a few perfect ones for garnishing. Sweeten the raspberry purée with the castor sugar, then blend them into the cream mixture. Transfer to a serving dish and chill. Just before serving, decorate with a few whole, hulled raspberries.

TALATTOURI

½ pint natural yogurt
1 cucumber
2 tbs finely chopped
    mint
salt, pepper
2 cloves garlic
1 tsp oil

Add the crushed garlic to the yogurt and stir well. Peel and finely chop the cucumber. Blend together the mint, cucumber, yogurt and a good pinch of freshly milled coarse salt. Blend in the oil and serve very cold, with slices of sausage, hardboiled eggs or prawns.

BEERY BEEF CASSEROLE

2 lb chuck steak
2 large carrots
2 large onions
2 oz butter
1 clove garlic
salt, pepper
1 bay leaf
sprig thyme
sprig parsley
pinch nutmeg
1 oz flour
½ pint brown ale

Dice the meat and season it with salt and pepper. Heat the butter, and fry the meat quickly in this until brown all over. Add the peeled and sliced onions, crushed garlic and sliced carrots and fry in the same butter for a few minutes. Sprinkle in the flour, stir well, then gradually add the beer, ½ pint water or beef stock, salt, pepper, nutmeg, bay leaf, thyme and parsley. Bring to the boil, then transfer to a casserole dish and cook in a moderate oven for 1½ hours.

POTATO AND ONION PUREE

1 lb potatoes
2 lb onions
½ gill milk
2 oz butter
salt, pepper
nutmeg

Peel and slice the potatoes and onions. Boil them, together, in salted water until cooked. Drain and liquidize them, or press them thoroughly with a potato ricer. Return them to the heat for a few minutes, to evaporate any remaining water. Blend in the butter, salt, pepper and a pinch of grated nutmeg. Finally, blend in the heated milk. Stir well before serving.

BRANDY ROLL

½ lb butter
½ lb castor sugar
3 tbs cocoa
3 oz almonds
1½ tbs brandy
12 oz digestive biscuits
2 eggs

Soften the butter. Blend in the sugar, cocoa and well-beaten eggs. Beat the mixture until it has a smooth creamy consistency. Toast the almonds under the grill and chop them finely. Add them to the cream mixture together with the brandy. Crush the biscuits, either in a liquidizer, or wrapped in a tea towel and crushed with a rolling pin. Add these crumbs to the rest of the ingredients and mix well. Empty the mixture on to a large sheet of aluminium foil. Form it into a roll shape, twisting the ends of the foil tightly to keep it in shape. Chill for 4–5 hours. Serve cut into slices, with pouring cream.

OVERNIGHT TOMATO SOUP

1 lb tomatoes
1 lb onions
1 oz bacon
1 pint stock
2 cloves
salt, pepper
sugar
1 dess sage
1 dess tomato
ketchup
1 bay leaf
sprig parsley

Peel and slice the onions. Cut the bacon into small pieces. Toss it in a large pan until the fat starts to melt. Add the onions (and more fat or oil if needed) and allow to simmer until they begin to soften. Add the skinned and seeded tomatoes and cook for 2 more minutes. Add the remaining ingredients, bring to the boil, cover and transfer to the oven, Gas Reg ¼ or 150–165 deg. F. for 8–10 hours. Remove the herbs and liquidize the soup before serving. This is a long, slow-cooking soup, which will cook happily, undisturbed, overnight or during the day. Put into the oven at the same time as a rich meaty casserole and a milk pudding, it would provide a good, hot meal when you returned from a day's outing, and would not suffer in the least if you were an hour or two late.

MINCED VEAL ESCALOPES

1 lb minced raw veal
2 tbs parsley
1 small shallot
½ lemon
salt, pepper
1 clove garlic
1 egg
flour
2 tbs oil
1 oz butter
3 tbs vermouth
3 tbs beef or chicken
  stock

Blend together the veal, crushed garlic, finely chopped parsley, chopped shallot and the grated rind of ½ lemon. Season with 2 tsp salt, a good sprinkling of black pepper and the juice of ½ lemon. Stir in the beaten egg. Flour the hands and form the mixture into 8 balls, of equal size. Roll them in flour and allow them to stand in a cool place for 1 hour. Then roll them lightly with a floured rolling pin, to a thickness of ½ inch. Dust them well with flour. Heat the oil and butter in a large, thick frying pan. When really hot, add the minced escalopes and cook them for 2 minutes on each side. Add the vermouth and allow to bubble for 2 minutes, then reduce the heat and add the stock. Allow to simmer gently for 8–10 minutes. Serve with lemon quarters.

PEA PUREE

2 lb peas
salt, pepper
sprig mint
1 oz butter
3 tbs double cream

Shell the peas. Boil them in salted water for 30–35 minutes, until very tender. Drain them, then liquidize or press them through a sieve. Blend in the butter, cream, salt, pepper and a little finely chopped fresh mint. Reheat gently without allowing to boil.

HIGHLAND PEACHES

4 large peaches
2 lemons
2 tbs clear honey
2 tbs whisky
1 gill double cream

Peel the peaches, by plunging them into boiling water for 1 minute, then rubbing off the skins. Slice the peaches into a glass serving bowl. Gently heat together the honey and strained juice of 2 lemons. When the honey has completely melted, add the whisky. Stir well and pour this mixture over the sliced peaches. Chill before serving with whipped cream.

EGG MOUSSE

6 eggs
½ pint double cream
4 tbs liquid aspic jelly
Worcester sauce
salt, pepper

Hardboil the eggs. Shell them under cold running water. Sieve the yolks; chop the whites very finely. Add the aspic jelly to the yolks, stirring well. Lightly whip the cream. Blend together the yolks, cream and whites, seasoning with a dash of Worcester sauce, salt and pepper. Chill before serving. A teaspoonful of curry powder could be added for a change.

STEAK AND KIDNEY PIE

½ lb calf's or ox kidney
1 lb chuck steak
salt, pepper
½ oz flour
1 oz butter
2 large onions
1 bay leaf
6 oz mushrooms
6–8 oz short or flaky
    pastry
½–¾ pint beef stock

Skin and slice the kidney, discarding any nerves or fat. Dust it with flour. Heat the butter in a frying pan, and fry the floured kidney in this quickly for 2 minutes. then transfer it to an ovenware dish. Dice the beef, dust it with flour and fry it in the same way as the kidney, until lightly browned all over. Peel, slice and fry the onions in the same way, mixing together the kidney, beef and onions in the ovenware dish. Season well with salt and pepper, add the bay leaf, and cover level with boiling stock. Cover with a lid and allow to cook in a moderate oven for 1½–2 hours. Toss the sliced mushrooms in butter and add them to the steak and kidney for the last 10 minutes of cooking. When cooked, allow the stew to cool. Cover it with a good short or flaky pastry and bake until golden in a hot oven.

DANISH BEETROOT

5–6 small raw beetroot
soft brown sugar
wine vinegar
2 tbs redcurrant jelly

Wash the beetroot. Boil them in salted water until tender. Drain them well, peel them while still hot. Slice them thinly. Arrange a layer of beetroot slices in the bottom of a serving dish.* Sprinkle with a dessertspoonful of sugar, then a tablespoonful of wine vinegar. Add another layer of beetroot, then sugar and vinegar, and continue until all the beetroot is used. Heat the redcurrant jelly until melted, and pour it over the beetroot. Allow to cool and stand for at least an hour before serving.

*Because of its pretty colour, beetroot looks particularly good when served in a glass dish.

PINEAPPLE BRULEE

1 medium pineapple
trifle sponge cakes
2 tbs rum
2 oz demerara sugar

Arrange the trifle sponge cakes in the bottom of a soufflé dish. Sprinkle them with the rum and allow to soak for 1 hour. Cut the pineapple into smallish pieces, discarding all the fibrous parts. Arrange the pineapple on top of the sponges. Sprinkle thickly with demerara sugar and grill until the sugar has caramelized. Serve hot.

POIREAUX A LA PROVENCALE

2 lb thin young leeks
½ lb tomatoes
1 lemon
2 tbs olive oil
black olives
salt, pepper

Cut the leeks into 2 inch lengths, using only the white part. Wash them well. Heat the oil in a sauté pan. Add the leeks. Cover the pan and allow to simmer for 10 minutes. Add the skinned, halved tomatoes, the juice of 1 lemon, salt, pepper, a few black olives and a small piece of lemon peel. Allow to cook for a further 10 minutes, uncovered. Discard the lemon peel before serving.

LAMB AND KIDNEY HOTPOT

6 lean lamb chops
6 lambs kidneys
10 medium potatoes
1 large onion
salt, pepper
½ pint stock

Trim the chops of all fat and bone. Skin and halve the kidneys. Peel and slice the potatoes and onion. Place a layer of potatoes in the bottom of a deep ovenware dish. Follow this with a layer of chops, then onion, then kidney. Continue these alternate layers, seasoning each layer to taste, until the dish is full, ending with potatoes. Pour over the stock. Cover with a sheet of buttered greaseproof paper and bake in a moderate oven for 2 hours, removing the paper for a final 30 minutes.

BRAISED CHICORY

1½ lb chicory
2 rashers bacon
1 lemon
2 oz butter

Trim the outer leaves of the chicory. Butter an ovenware dish. Arrange the chicory in it. Sprinkle with salt and pepper. Dice the bacon and add it to the chicory. Cover with the juice of 1 lemon. Cover with a lid, or a piece of foil, and bake in a low oven for 1 hour, turning the chicory from time to time. Serve sprinkled with finely chopped parsley.

GOOSEBERRY PUDDING

1 lb gooseberries
3–4 oz sugar
1 oz butter
4 oz sponge cake

Do not bother to top and tail the gooseberries. Place them in a pan, together with the sugar and ¼ pint water. Bring to the boil and allow to simmer until tender, then press the fruit through a sieve. Butter an ovenware dish. Transform the cake into fine crumbs. Use half of them to line the base and sides of the buttered dish. Fill with the gooseberry purée, then cover with the remaining cake crumbs. Sprinkle with castor sugar and bake in a low oven until lightly browned. Serve hot with cream.

CRECY SOUP

2 onions
4 carrots
2 oz butter
1 oz rice
1½ pint chicken stock
salt, pepper
pinch sugar
mixed herbs

Peel and slice the onions and carrots. Melt 1 oz butter in a thick pan. Cook the onions gently until soft and lightly brown. Add the carrots and rice. Stir well, then pour in the boiling stock. Season with salt, pepper and a pinch of sugar. Add a sprig of thyme and parsley or a pinch of dried mixed herbs. Allow to simmer gently for 1½ hours. Liquidize, or rub the mixture through a sieve. Reheat, and blend in the remaining butter just before serving. This soup has a thick almost porridge consistency, and a gentle flavour.

BEEF SLICES WITH GARLIC

1½ lb chuck steak
1 lb tomatoes
oil
5 cloves garlic
2 tbs chopped parsley
2 tbs vinegar
salt, pepper
6 tbs dry white wine
    or sherry
beef stock

Cut the meat into fairly thin slices. Toss them in seasoned flour, and fry them in hot oil until brown all over. Transfer them to an ovenware dish. Add the peeled, sliced tomatoes, finely chopped garlic, parsley, salt and pepper. To the oil left in the pan, add the vinegar and wine, and stir well over the heat for a few minutes. Pour this over the meat, and add sufficient stock to barely cover. Cover with a lid and cook in a low oven for 1½ hours.

SPAGHETTI WITH PARMESAN

½ lb spaghetti
salt, pepper
3 oz unsalted butter
2 oz grated parmesan
    cheese

Have ready a large pan of boiling salted water. Add the spaghetti, coiling it round the pan as it softens. Allow to boil for 11–12 minutes, then drain it well. Just before serving blend in more salt and pepper, the butter and the grated parmesan. Toss well.

PEACH CREME BRULEE

4 large fresh peaches
1 tbs castor sugar
2 tbs brandy or liqueur
½ pint double cream
6 oz demerara sugar

Plunge the peaches into boiling water for 1 minute only, then rub off their skins. Slice the peaches and arrange them in an ovenproof soufflé dish. Sprinkle them with the castor sugar and brandy. Whip the cream until stiff. Spread this over the peaches and allow to stand in the refrigerator overnight. Spread the demerara sugar over the surface, to a depth of about ½ inch, then pop the dish under the grill for a few minutes, until the sugar caramelizes. Serve at once.

BAKED COURGETTES

4 medium or 8 tiny
  courgettes
1 large onion
4 tomatoes
1 clove garlic
salt, pepper
pinch mixed herbs
2 tbs fresh breadcrumbs
½ oz grated Parmesan
  cheese
1½ oz butter

Heat 1 oz butter in a pan. Add the peeled and finely chopped onion and crushed garlic and cook until soft but not brown. Add the peeled and chopped tomatoes, salt, pepper and a pinch of mixed herbs. Allow to cook for 5 minutes. Top and tail the courgettes and halve them lengthwise. Plunge them into boiling, salted water for 2 minutes, then drain them well. Scoop out a little of the flesh from the centre of each, chop it, add it to the cooked tomato and fill each hollowed courgette with this savoury mixture. Top each with breadcrumbs and cheese, previously mixed together. Arrange the courgettes in a buttered baking dish, put a knob of butter on each and bake in a moderate oven for 15 minutes. Finally pop them under the grill to brown, before serving.

SALMON MOUSSE

1 lb fresh salmon
1 pint aspic jelly
4 tbs mayonnaise
salt, pepper
½ lemon
3 inches of cucumber
a few prawns
watercress

Wrap the salmon in greaseproof paper. Barely cover with boiling salted water, and allow to simmer very gently for 10 minutes. Allow it to cool in the water. Prepare the aspic, according to the instructions on the packet, using the water in which the salmon was cooked in place of water. Allow the aspic to cool. When it is just beginning to set, arrange a few prawns and slices of cucumber in a decorative pattern in the bottom of a mould. Carefully cover with a thin layer of the setting aspic, and place in the refrigerator to set. In a bowl place the mayonnaise, 2 tbs finely chopped cucumber and the flaked, cooked salmon. Blend in the juice of ½ lemon, salt, pepper and the remaining aspic. Fill the mould with this mixture and chill. Before serving, turn the mould out on to a plate, and surround it with sprigs of watercress.

ORANGE AND WATERCRESS SALAD

3 bunches watercress
2 large oranges
salt, pepper
5 tbs olive oil
2 tbs vinegar

Wash the watercress and tear it into bite-size sprigs. Drain it well, then dry it in a cloth or kitchen paper. Peel the oranges, and remove all the pith. Cut the oranges into thin rounds. Whisk together the oil, vinegar, salt and pepper. Pour this over the watercress and oranges and toss well.

DUKE OF CAMBRIDGE TART

½ lb short pastry
*4 oz chopped mixed
  candied peel
6 oz unsalted butter
6 oz castor sugar
2 large eggs

Line a flan ring with short pastry. Cover the base with the candied peel. Put the butter, sugar and eggs in a thick saucepan. Mix them together over a gentle heat, stirring all the time. As soon as boiling point is reached, pour this mixture over the peel. Transfer to a moderate oven for 40–45 minutes, after which time the filling should be brown and crinkly.

*For a luxury version, soak the candied peel in liqueur or brandy before use.

OMELETTE LYONNAISE

1 large onion
5 eggs
salt, pepper
1 oz butter
1 tbs double cream

Heat the butter in an omelette pan. Add the onion, peeled and cut into thin rings. Allow to cook until soft and pale golden in colour. Beat together the eggs, cream, salt and pepper. Pour this over the onions and allow to cook gently until set. Fold the omelette in half, and cut it into four portions. Serve with thin slices of smoked ham.

KIDNEYS AND MUSHROOMS

1 lb lamb's kidneys
8 oz mushrooms
1 small glass port or
  marsala
1 clove garlic
2 oz butter
1 oz flour
parsley
salt, pepper

Slice, season and flour the kidneys. Heat the butter in a large frying pan. Add the kidneys and toss them until seared all over. Pour in the port or marsala and allow to bubble for a few minutes. Cover level with water and allow to simmer gently for 40 minutes. Add the sliced mushrooms and 1 crushed clove of garlic. Simmer for a further 15 minutes. Serve sprinkled with parsley.

TOMATOES STUFFED WITH PEAS

4 very large tomatoes
2 spring onions
4 tbs cooked peas
4 tbs mayonnaise

Halve the tomatoes across. Scoop out the seeds. Finely chop the spring onions and blend them with the cooked peas. Fill each hollowed tomato half with a spoonful of these onion-flavoured peas, and top with a dollop of mayonnaise.

STONE CREAM

1 lemon
½ pint double cream
2 egg whites
2 tbs sherry or vermouth
2 oz castor sugar
½ oz gelatine
cherry jam

Dissolve the gelatine in 1 gill hot water, stirring it over a very low heat. When dissolved blend in the grated rind of 1 lemon, the sugar and sherry or vermouth. Whip the cream stiffly. Whip the egg whites stiffly. Blend the egg whites into the cream. Add the strained gelatine, and stir well. Place a spoonful of cherry jam in the bottom of each serving dish. Cover with the cream and chill before serving.

LACED TOMATO JUICE

1 pint tomato juice
1½ tbs whisky
salt, pepper
Worcester sauce

Blend together the tomato juice, salt, pepper, whisky and a dash of Worcester sauce. Serve piping hot in lemon tea glasses.

LAMB AND APPLE PIE

8 lamb cutlets
4 eating apples
salt, pepper
2 onions
soft brown sugar
½ lb short pastry

Trim the fat from the cutlets. Peel and slice the onions. Peel, core and slice the apples. Fill a pie dish with alternate layers of cutlets, onion and apple, seasoning each layer with salt, pepper and a pinch of brown sugar. Cover with a cupful of cold water and bake in a moderate oven for ¾–1 hour, by which time the meat should be quite tender. Cover with a short pastry lid, prick some holes in the top and bake in a hot oven for a further 15–20 minutes.

POIREAUX AU GRATIN

10–12 small leeks
½ pint basic white sauce
6 tbs grated cheese
2 oz butter
2 oz fresh white bread-
   crumbs

Cut the leeks into 2 inch pieces, using only the white parts. Clean them well, then boil in salted water for 10–15 minutes. Drain well. Arrange them in an ovenware dish. Heat the white sauce, blend in 3 oz grated cheese, and stir well until melted. Pour this sauce over the leeks. Blend together the remaining cheese and breadcrumbs. Cover the sauce with this mixture and dot with large nuts of butter. Brown in a hot oven, or under the grill.

MERINGUES ANGELIQUE

3 egg whites
salt
6 oz castor sugar
½ pint double cream
½ lb raspberries

Beat the egg whites, with a pinch of salt, until absolutely stiff. Fold in the sugar gently, with a metal spoon. Take 2 baking trays. Turn them upside down and place a sheet of rice paper on each. Brush the rice paper lightly with olive oil. Scoop large spoonfuls of the meringue mixture onto the oiled rice paper, and bake in a very low oven, Reg. 1, for 3–4 hours. Whip the cream. Fold the raspberries into it, together with castor sugar if needed. Sandwich together the cold meringues with this raspberry cream.

CREAM OF CUCUMBER SOUP

1 cucumber
1 oz butter
½ oz flour
1 pint chicken stock
salt, pepper
½ pint milk
1 egg
4 tbs double cream

Peel and halve the cucumber. Scoop out and discard its seeds. Dice the cucumber flesh. Melt the butter in a thick pan. Sprinkle in the flour, stir well and gradually add the boiling stock, stirring all the time. Season with salt and pepper. Add the diced cucumber and allow to simmer for 10–15 minutes, by which time the cucumber should be quite tender. Liquidize, or rub the mixture through a sieve. Return it to the pan, reheat and blend in the hot milk. Whisk together the egg and cream. Remove the pan from the heat, and beat this creamy mixture into the soup. Serve at once.

BURGUNDY BEEF

1 lb lean stewing beef
1 oz butter
1 oz flour
3 rashers bacon
3 large onions
2 cloves garlic
½ pint red wine
salt, pepper
4 oz mushrooms
beef stock

Cut the beef into smallish pieces. Heat the butter in a thick saucepan. Add the beef, diced bacon and peeled, sliced onions. Toss well over the heat until lightly browned. Stir in the flour, and add the finely chopped garlic. Stir well, then gradually add the wine, stirring all the time. Also add sufficient stock, or water, to barely cover the meat. Season with salt and pepper. Cover with a lid and allow to cook gently, either in the oven or on top of the stove, for 1½ hours. Then add the sliced mushrooms, stir well and continue to cook for a further 30 minutes.*

*This would make an excellent pie. Simply allow it to cool, cover it with a good rich short or flaky pastry and bake it in a hot oven until golden.

FRENCH BEANS WITH ALMONDS

1 lb French beans
1½ oz butter
salt, pepper
2 oz flaked almonds
½ gill chicken stock

Heat the butter in a thick pan. Add the beans, finely sliced, salt and pepper. Allow to cook for 5 minutes, stirring from time to time, then add the stock, cover and allow to simmer for 8–10 minutes. Blend in the almonds, stir well over the heat for 2 minutes, then serve, draining off any liquid which may remain.

CARAMEL ORANGES

3 large oranges
1 gill fresh orange or
 tangerine juice
4 oz castor sugar

for caramel:
2 tbs water
3 oz castor sugar

Peel the oranges. Slice them into rounds, discarding any pith or pips. Boil together the orange juice and sugar for 15 minutes. Allow it to cool, then pour it over the sliced oranges. Make the caramel in a thick pan by gently heating together the sugar and water, without stirring. As soon as the caramel takes on a rich brown colour, remove the pan from the heat and pour the caramel over the oranges. Chill well. Just before serving, break up the caramel into smallish pieces, with a knife.

GLOBE ARTICHOKES WITH LEMON BUTTER

4 globe artichokes
1 lemon
salt, pepper
4 oz unsalted butter

Trim the stalks of the artichokes. Bring to the boil a large pan of salted water. Add the artichokes and ½ lemon. Bring back to the boil and allow to simmer, half-covered, for about 35 minutes. The artichokes are ready when a leaf comes off easily if pulled. In a small pan heat the butter, salt, pepper, the grated rind and strained juice of ½ lemon. Serve this hot lemony butter with the artichokes.

DUCK STUFFED WITH APPLES

1 duck
3 cooking apples
2 tsp sugar
water
1 oz butter
cinnamon

for sauce:
1 oz butter
1 tbs sugar
3 tbs wine vinegar
salt, pepper

Peel the apples and cut them into irregular pieces. Barely cover them with water, add a small piece of cinnamon (or a pinch of ground cinnamon), and the sugar and cook gently until reduced to a pulp. Stuff the trussed duck with this apple mixture. Heat 1 oz butter in a frying pan, and sear the duck all over with this until golden. Meanwhile, melt 1 oz butter in a small pan, add 1 tbs sugar, the vinegar, salt and pepper. Bring this to the boil and allow to cook quickly for 5 minutes. Pour this over the duck, cover with a tight-fitting lid, or foil, and roast in a moderate oven for 1–1¼ hours.

GARLICKED SPINACH

2 lb spinach
2 oz butter
2 garlic cloves
¾ pint basic white sauce
salt, pepper

Heat the butter in a large pan. Add the crushed garlic cloves and allow to cook for 2 minutes. Carefully wash and pick over the spinach, draining it in a colander. Stir it into the garlic butter, and allow to cook for 8–10 minutes, stirring all the time. Liquidize the spinach or pass it through a mouli. Add the resulting purée to the white sauce, and reheat thoroughly. Check the seasoning.

CHOCOLATE CAKE

4 oz plain chocolate
4 oz castor sugar
2 tbs flour
3 oz unsalted butter
3 eggs

for icing:
3 oz plain chocolate
4 sugar lumps
2 tbs water
1 oz butter

Melt the chocolate, either in the oven or in a bowl over a pan of boiling water. Blend in the softened butter, flour, sugar and beaten egg yolks. Whisk the egg whites stiffly, and fold them gently but thoroughly into the mixture. Transfer to a buttered cake tin and bake in a moderate oven for 40 minutes. A fine crust will have formed on top, and the inside will appear uncooked, but do not worry. Allow it to cool slightly, then turn it upside down on a cooling rack, and allow it to cool completely. Prepare the icing by melting the chocolate, together with the water and sugar lumps. When the mixture is absolutely smooth, blend in the softened butter. Use this icing while it is still warm, but not hot.

GREEN PEA SOUP

2 lb peas
1 lettuce heart
4 oz butter
2 pints water or stock
salt, pepper
sugar

Heat the butter in a thick pan. Add the shredded lettuce, shelled peas, 2 sugar lumps, 2 tsp salt and plenty of freshly milled black pepper. Cover the pan and allow to cook gently for 10 minutes. Add the boiling water or stock and allow to simmer until the peas are cooked. Liquidize, or rub the mixture through a sieve.

FILLET STEAKS WITH CROUTONS

4 thick fillet steaks
4 tbs chopped mixed
    parsley, chervil, basil,
    mint and tarragon
2 oz butter
1 lemon
4 tbs brandy
4 rounds French bread

Trim the steaks of fat, rub them all over with the herbs and allow to stand for 30 minutes, for the flavour of the herbs to penetrate the meat. Heat the butter in a thick pan. Cook the steaks quickly on both sides. Transfer the steaks to a second, fatless pan, sprinkle them on both sides with lemon juice and continue to cook them to the required degree of 'doneness'. Meanwhile, fry the slices of French bread in the first frying pan. To serve, arrange a cooked steak on each round of fried bread, and pour any remaining butter over.*

*You may need to heat more butter to pour over the steaks if the French bread absorbed the first lot.

FRENCH BEANS WITH TOMATOES

¾ lb French beans
4–5 large tomatoes
salt, pepper
1½ oz butter
1 clove garlic

Heat the butter in a thick pan. Add the crushed garlic and allow to cook for 2–3 minutes. Add the beans, finely sliced, and toss well for 5 minutes. Add the tomatoes, peeled and quartered, and season well with salt and pepper. Stir well, cover the pan and allow to cook for 10–15 minutes. The tomatoes should provide sufficient liquid to prevent burning, but if not, add a little stock or water.

CHOCOLATE BRANDY WHIP

4 oz plain chocolate
4 eggs
vanilla essence
½ oz butter
1 tbs brandy
single cream

Melt the chocolate in a low oven, or in a basin over hot water. Remove from the heat. Beat the egg yolks. Add this beaten mixture to the chocolate gradually, beating well between each addition. Blend in 1 tsp boiling water and a few drops of vanilla essence. Cut the butter into tiny pieces and beat them into the mixture. Add the brandy, stir well, then allow the mixture to cool. Beat the egg whites until stiff and peaky. Fold them into the chocolate mixture with a metal spoon. Make sure that no traces of white remain. Chill before serving with pouring cream.

FLAMICHE

½ lb short pastry
12 thin leeks
2 rashers bacon
½ pint white sauce
½ gill single cream
salt, pepper
1 oz butter

Line a flan ring with the pastry, and allow it to stand in the refrigerator while preparing the filling. Heat the butter in a thick pan. Slice the leeks very thinly, using only the white parts. Sauté them in the butter until soft but not coloured. Add the leeks and the butter in which they were cooked to the white sauce. Blend in the cream, finely chopped and fried bacon, salt and pepper. Pour the mixture into the flan ring and bake in a moderate oven for 20 minutes.

PORK CHOPS WITH CRANBERRIES

4 lean pork chops
1 gill red wine
1 tbs oil
1 cupful cranberries
flour
4 oz honey
1 gill water
salt, pepper

Heat the oil in a frying pan. Brown the chops on both sides in this. Sprinkle in a little flour, then add the red wine and water, stirring all the time. Season to taste. Transfer the mixture to a casserole. Put the cranberries into a basin, add the honey, and lightly crush the berries with a spoon. Pour this mixture over the chops, cover the dish and cook in a moderate oven for 1 hour.

CABBAGE AND TOMATO SALAD

1 cabbage heart
5–6 tomatoes
2 oz black olives
salt, pepper
6 tbs olive oil
2 tbs lemon juice

Shred the cabbage heart finely. Add the tomatoes, peeled and roughly chopped. Stone the olives and add these to the cabbage and tomatoes. Whisk together the oil, lemon juice, salt and pepper. Pour this over the vegetables and toss well before serving.

MELON SALAD

as many different varieties
of melon as possible
port or sherry
sugar to taste

Simply cut the different varieties of melon into neat balls, or bite-size cubes. Sprinkle them with port or sherry and chill well before serving. Melon's powerful smell transmits itself all too easily to everything in the refrigerator, so make sure that it is well sealed before chilling. Or, chill it by surrounding its bowl with crushed ice.

STUFFED EGGS

4 eggs
2 spring onions
2 tbs mayonnaise
1 dess curry powder
salt, pepper
chopped parsley

Hardboil the eggs. Cool and shell them. Halve them lengthwise and scoop out the yolks. Mash them with a fork, and blend in the mayonnaise, finely chopped spring onions, parsley, curry powder, salt and pepper. When well mixed, fill the cavity in each egg half with this savoury mixture. Serve on a bed of shredded lettuce and sprigs of watercress.

PHEASANT WITH CELERY AND CREAM

1 pheasant
½ pint game or chicken stock
1 gill port or marsala
½ pint cream
1 egg yolk
salt, pepper
4 oz butter
2 rashers lean bacon
2 heads celery
1 tsp chopped parsley
1 tsp chopped lovage

Heat the butter in a frying pan, and brown the pheasant all over in it. Transfer it to an ovenware casserole and add the diced bacon, stock, herbs and port. Season to taste. Cover and allow to cook in a moderate oven for 30 minutes, before adding the celery, cut into rounds. Continue cooking for a further 45 minutes, then arrange the pheasant and celery on a warm serving dish. Beat together the egg yolk and cream. Gradually stir it into the hot gravy, and reheat gently, without allowing it to boil. Serve this sauce with the pheasant and celery.

FRENCH BEANS WITH MUSHROOMS

¾ lb French beans
½ lb button mushrooms
2 oz butter
salt, pepper
1 clove garlic
½ gill chicken stock

Heat the butter in a thick pan. Add the crushed garlic and allow to cook for 2 minutes, then add the French beans, finely sliced. Toss for 5 minutes over a gentle heat, then add the sliced mushrooms, salt and pepper. Allow to cook for 5 minutes, then add a little stock, cover the pan and allow to cook until the beans are tender. Drain off any excess liquid before serving.

CREAMY CHERRY FLAN

½ lb short pastry
1 lb cherries
2 oz castor sugar
1 gill double cream
1 egg yolk

Line a flan ring with short pastry. Stone the cherries and arrange them, very close together, in the flan ring. Sprinkle with the sugar. Beat together the cream and egg yolk. Pour this over the cherries. Bake in a moderate oven for 30–35 minutes, or until the cream is lightly set.

MUSHROOM SALAD

¾ lb button mushrooms
parsley
6 tbs oil
2 tbs wine vinegar
salt, pepper
½ tsp French mustard
1 clove garlic

Clean but do not peel the mushrooms. If very tiny, leave them whole, otherwise halve them. Place them in a plastic container which has an airtight lid, or a glass jar with a screw top. Whisk together the oil, vinegar, crushed garlic, salt, pepper and mustard. Pour this over the mushrooms, together with a handful of finely chopped parsley. Cover with the lid and allow the mushrooms to marinade for at least 2 hours, turning the container upside down from time to time, to ensure that every mushroom has its fair share of dressing. Serve with thin slices of boiled ham or tongue.

GAMMON COOKED IN SHERRY

4 gammon steaks
1 oz butter
½ lemon
1 gill sherry
1 dess flour
pepper

Heat the butter in a frying pan and stir in the flour. Cook for a moment or two, then gradually add the sherry and lemon juice. The sauce should not be too thick, so you may have to add a little water. Season with pepper only. When the sauce is well blended add the gammon steaks, and allow to simmer for 15 minutes.

RED CABBAGE WITH APPLE

1 medium red cabbage
1 large onion
1 large cooking apple
1 oz butter
2 tbs wine vinegar
salt, pepper
1 tbs soft brown sugar
2 tbs beef stock

Shred the cabbage finely, discarding any tough or damaged outer leaves. Heat the butter in a large pan. Add the shredded cabbage, finely sliced onion and apple, salt, pepper, vinegar, sugar and stock. Stir well and cover with a close-fitting lid. Allow to cook gently for 40–45 minutes, stirring from time to time. Most of the liquid should have been absorbed by the end of the cooking period.

CARAMEL ICE CREAM

3 eggs
½ pint double cream
3 tbs castor sugar
1 vanilla pod

for caramel:
2 oz castor sugar

Put the cream and vanilla pod in a pan and bring to the boil. Remove from the heat immediately and allow to cool. Remove the vanilla pod, which may be used again, if dried carefully. Stir 3 oz castor sugar into the cream then blend this mixture with the well-beaten eggs. Heat this mixture gently in a double pan, stirring all the time and not allowing to boil. As soon as it begins to thicken remove the pan from the heat and allow to cool. Heat the remaining 2 oz castor sugar in a very thick pan until it turns to the colour of dark honey and smells strongly of caramel. Pour it into the custard, stir well and when absolutely cold, pour it into an ice-making tray. Cover it with foil and freeze at maximum temperature for 3 hours, agitating it with a fork twice during the freezing period.

SPLIT PEA SOUP

1 teacupful split peas
1 small carrot
1 onion
salt, pepper
1 bay leaf
¼ tsp Worcester sauce
1½ pints beef stock
2 rashers bacon

Wash and drain the peas. Peel and dice the carrot. Grate the onion and chop the bacon. Put all the ingredients into a pan, bring to the boil, cover and transfer to the oven, Gas Mark ¼ or 150–165 deg. F. for 8–10 hours. Remove the bay leaf before serving. This can be cooked overnight, or during the day, whichever is most convenient, but needs no attention during cooking time, and will not spoil if left for an hour or two more than the prescribed time.

COTELETTES D'AGNEAU EN PAPILLOTES

8 lamb cutlets
1 oz flour
salt, pepper
3 oz butter
3 medium onions
2 cloves garlic
3 tomatoes
3 tbs white wine or
    vermouth
1 tbs chopped parsley
2 oz ham

Trim the cutlets. Coat them in seasoned flour. Fry them in butter for 12–15 minutes, turning them occasionally. Transfer them to a dish. Finely chop the onions and garlic and fry them until golden brown. Add the peeled, sliced tomatoes, the chopped parsley, wine and seasoning. Allow to simmer until reduced to a thick pulp. Remove from the heat and allow to cool, then blend in the ham, cut into small pieces. Cut out 8 heart shapes of greaseproof paper, each larger than the cutlets. Spread each paper heart with butter and place some of the tomato mixture on each. Arrange a cutlet on each, then top with more of the tomato mixture. Fold up the paper carefully, so that none of the precious juices can escape. Bake on a greased tray in a moderate oven for 15–20 minutes.

ASPARAGUS WITH LEMON SAUCE

1 lb asparagus
2 oz butter
2 egg yolks
1 lemon
salt, pepper

Scrape the asparagus, tie it in a bundle and cook it in boiling salted water, tips just out of the water, for about 20 minutes, or until tender. Drain it well, then keep it hot while preparing the sauce. Melt the butter. Put the egg yolks in a small thick pan. Gradually add the melted butter, stirring all the time. When the sauce thickens, season with salt and pepper and add the strained juice of the lemon. Untie the asparagus and arrange it on a heated dish. Surround it with lemon slices and serve the sauce separately.

FRESH FIGS

10–12 fresh ripe figs
½ gill port
1 tbs Curaçao
½ pint double cream

Peel and slice the figs. Place them in a glass bowl surrounded by crushed ice. Stir in the port and Curaçao and allow to stand for 30 minutes. Just before serving, pour the cream over them and, stir well.

SMOKED TROUT PATE

1 smoked trout
1 thick slice bread
⅓ cupful olive oil
1 large lemon
salt, pepper
1 small onion

Skin and bone the trout. Soak a thick, crustless slice of bread in water for 10 minutes. Squeeze out the surplus moisture, then pound together the trout flesh and the bread, until well amalgamated. Add the grated onion. Gradually add the oil, stirring all the time. Season to taste, and add as much lemon juice as required to give the desired flavour.

MEAT LOAF WITH EGG

1 lb minced beef
2 eggs
1 clove garlic
1 small onion
salt, pepper
parsley
1 hardboiled egg
1 oz boiled ham
mixed herbs, fresh if
    possible

Mince the beef twice. Blend in the beaten eggs, salt, pepper, crushed garlic, grated onion and plenty of finely chopped parsley. Blend together well. Flatten the mixture into an oblong shape on a floured board. Peel and chop the hardboiled egg. Mix it together with the chopped boiled ham, salt, pepper and mixed herbs. Spread this mixture on top of the meat, then roll it up, Swiss-roll style. Wrap it in buttered foil, and cook in a fairly low oven for 1½ hours, adding a little stock if it appears to be drying too much.

GLOBE ARTICHOKES WITH BUTTER

4 globe artichokes
salt, pepper
½ lemon
2 oz butter

Trim the stalks of the artichokes. Bring to the boil a large panful of salted water. Add the artichokes and ½ lemon. Bring back to the boil and allow to simmer until the artichokes are cooked. This will vary, of course, according to the size and condition of the artichoke, but should take between 25–35 minutes. The artichoke is cooked when a leaf can be detached cleanly and easily. Drain the artichokes, head downmost in a colander. Heat the butter, season it with plenty of freshly ground black pepper and serve this with the hot, cooked artichokes.

APPLE CREAM

1 lb Bramley apples
3 oz brown sugar
½ pint water
1 tbs Benedictine or
    brandy
1 gill double cream

Boil together the sugar and water, until the sugar has quite melted. Peel, core and slice the apples. Simmer them in this syrup until soft. Liquidize, or press them through a sieve. Flavour with the Benedictine or brandy. Allow to cool. Blend in the whipped cream. Serve very cold.

AVOCADO WITH CHIVES AND VINAIGRETTE

2 avocado pears
6 tbs oil
2 tbs wine vinegar
½ tsp French mustard
salt, pepper
chives

Halve the avocado pears and discard the stones. Whisk together the oil, vinegar, salt, pepper and mustard. Pour a little of this into each cavity. Sprinkle each avocado with finely chopped chives.

CIDERED HAM

1½–2 lb piece of gammon
1 onion
cloves
cider
mixed herbs
moist brown sugar

Soak the gammon overnight in cold water. Rinse. Place it in a pan, and barely cover it with cider. Add the onion, studded with 2 cloves, and a pinch of mixed herbs. Bring to the boil. Transfer to a moderate oven and cook until tender, allowing 25 minutes per 1 lb. Peel off the skin, while still hot. Stud the surface of the gammon with cloves. Press on a thick layer of moist brown sugar. Bake until golden, moistening with more cider from time to time.

STUFFED AUBERGINES

2 large aubergines
1 onion
2 oz butter
2 oz white breadcrumbs
salt, pepper
2 bacon rashers
2 oz mushrooms
parsley

Halve the aubergines and scoop out the flesh—a grapefruit knife is quite useful for this operation. Chop the aubergine flesh and boil it in salted water for 5 minutes. In a second pan boil the skins in salted water for 10 minutes. Heat the butter in a frying pan. Add the peeled and sliced onion and allow to cook gently until tender, but not brown. Add the bacon, cut into pieces, and the sliced mushrooms. Allow to cook for a further 5 minutes, then stir in the breadcrumbs, salt, pepper, drained aubergine pulp and 1 tbs finely chopped parsley. Fill the drained aubergine skins with this mixture. Cover each with a layer of breadcrumbs, sprinkle with a little melted butter and cook in a moderate oven for 10–15 minutes.

REDCURRANT MOUSSE

1¼ lb redcurrants
10 oz sugar
1 gill double cream
2 egg whites

Stem the fruit. Wash it well, then place it in a pan with 2 tbs water. Allow to cook very gently, covered, until the fruit is soft, shaking the pan from time to time. Evaporate any surplus juice by boiling over a higher flame for a few minutes, without the lid. Remove the pan from the heat and stir in the sugar. Press the fruit through a nylon sieve with a wooden spoon. Chill the redcurrant purée. Whip the cream until stiff. Whip the egg whites until stiff. Fold the cream and egg whites into the redcurrant mixture, making sure that no traces of white remain. Chill before serving.

STUFFED TOMATOES

4 giant, or 8 medium
  tomatoes
3 oz brown or granary
  breadcrumbs
parsley
1 clove garlic
1 small onion
3 tbs oil
salt, pepper

Slice the tops off the tomatoes. Using a teaspoon, soften and scoop out the flesh. Heat 2 tbs oil in a pan. Add the crushed garlic and peeled, chopped onion, and fry until soft but not brown. Blend in the breadcrumbs, salt, pepper and plenty of finely chopped parsley. Fill the hollowed tomatoes with this mixture. Replace the tomato tops. Arrange the stuffed tomatoes in a shallow baking dish. Sprinkle with the remaining oil and bake in a moderate oven for 20–25 minutes.

ESCALOPES DE VEAU A LA CREME AUX CHAMPIGNONS

4 veal escalopes
salt, pepper
½ lemon
½ lb button mushrooms
1 clove garlic
1 gill double cream
parsley
1½ oz butter

Season the escalopes, on both sides, with salt, pepper and lemon juice. Heat the butter in a large frying pan. Cook the escalopes on both sides in the butter, until lightly browned. Add the finely sliced mushrooms, crushed garlic, more salt and pepper. Cover the pan and allow to cook gently for 10 minutes. Transfer the veal and mushrooms to a serving dish and keep them warm. To the juices left in the pan add the boiling cream. Stir well, and when thoroughly blended, pour this over the veal and mushrooms. Serve sprinkled with finely chopped parsley, or with sprigs of watercress.

GRATIN DE GRENOBLE

1 lb potatoes
2 turnips
1 clove garlic
½ pint double cream
salt, pepper
2 oz butter
nutmeg

Peel and grate the turnips. Butter an ovenware dish, and rub it well with the crushed garlic clove. Arrange the grated turnips in the bottom of the dish. Peel and thinly slice the potatoes and arrange them on top of the turnips. Season well with salt, pepper and freshly grated nutmeg.
Pour in the cream. Cover the surface with the melted butter. Cover the dish with a lid or foil, and bake in a moderate oven for 1½–1¾ hours.

STRAWBERRIES WITH RUM CREAM

1 lb strawberries
2 eggs
2 oz castor sugar
4 tbs rum
¾ pint whipped cream
sponge fingers

Beat the egg yolks. Blend in the sugar, rum and whipped cream. Arrange the strawberries in the bottom of a serving dish. Just before serving, cover them with whipped cream and surround with sponge fingers.

PRAWN COCKTAIL

8 oz peeled prawns
½ pint mayonnaise
lettuce
2 tbs tomato ketchup
1 tbs double cream
Worcester sauce

Arrange some shredded (torn with fingers not a knife) lettuce in 4 glass bowls or wine glasses. Pile the prawns on top. Blend together the mayonnaise, cream, ketchup and a dash of Worcester sauce. Pour this over the prawns and serve very cold.

BEEF OLIVES

4 thin slices lean beef
2 egg yolks
1 lemon
salt, pepper
1 oz butter
2 oz breadcrumbs
1 onion
thyme, parsley
¾ pint stock, beef or
   chicken
2 tbs flour

Flatten the beef slices. Blend together the breadcrumbs, grated onion, grated lemon rind, finely chopped herbs, egg yolks, salt and pepper. Spread this stuffing on each of the beef slices. Roll them up carefully and tie them securely with string or cotton. Heat the butter in a frying pan, and toss the beef olives in this quickly until brown all over. Then rub them in the flour and transfer them to an ovenware dish. Pour the stock over them, cover with a lid and allow to cook gently, in a moderate oven, for 1½ hours.

BEAN PUREE

½ lb haricot beans
salt, pepper
2 tbs olive oil
2 tbs finely chopped mint
1 clove garlic

Soak the beans in cold water for 4–5 hours. Drain them well, rinse them then transfer them to a saucepan. Cover them with cold water, bring to the boil and allow to cook gently until very soft. Drain, season with plenty of salt and pepper, and strain the beans through a sieve, or liquidize them. To the resulting purée add the crushed clove of garlic, olive oil and mint. Stir well and allow to cool. Serve cold, but not chilled.

ORANGE PUDDING

1 pint fresh orange juice
4 egg yolks
4 tbs sherry or vermouth
4 oz castor sugar
6 trifle sponge cakes
6 macaroons

Blend together the orange juice and sherry or vermouth. Beat together the egg yolks and sugar and stir this mixture into the orange juice. Fold in the finely crumbled cakes and macaroons. Pour the mixture into a buttered ovenware mould. Place it in a baking tray containing about 1 inch of water and bake in a moderately hot oven for 20 minutes. Allow to cool before serving with pouring cream.

SOUPE CATALANE

3 large onions
2 oz bacon
3 tomatoes
1 stalk celery
3 pints beef stock
2 potatoes
thyme, parsley
salt, pepper
nutmeg
2 egg yolks
1 wineglass sherry
2 tbs oil

Heat the oil in a thick pan. Slice the onions thinly, and add them to the oil. Fry gently until golden brown, then add the chopped bacon, skinned and quartered tomatoes and diced celery. Stir over a gentle heat for a few minutes, then add the sherry. Bring to the boil, then add the boiling stock, diced, peeled potatoes, a sprig of thyme, a few sprigs of parsley and a pinch of grated nutmeg. Allow to simmer for 30 minutes. Break the egg yolks into a tureen, and add a few spoonfuls of the near-boiling soup. Beat well, then add the rest of the soup, stirring all the time. Serve at once, sprinkled with finely chopped parsley.

ROAST PORK WITH ORANGE

4 lb loin or leg of pork
1 tsp sage
salt, pepper
1 tbs redcurrant jelly
2 large oranges
1 gill sherry
water

Rub the pork all over with salt, pepper and dried sage. Put it in a baking tray together with a cupful of water, and roast in a moderate oven allowing 30 minutes per 1 lb. Three quarters of an hour before cooking is complete remove the meat from the oven, and pour off any excess fat. Sprinkle the meat with the grated rind of 1 orange. To the gravy add the juice of 1 orange, the redcurrant jelly and sherry. Season to taste. Cut the second orange into 4–5 segments, complete with skin. Arrange these round the joint, return to the oven and continue cooking until absolutely tender.

ROAST PARSNIPS

2 lb parsnips
salt, pepper

Peel the parsnips and quarter them lengthwise. Boil them in salted water for 20 minutes. Drain well. Arrange the parsnips round the joint of pork 30 minutes before the meat is cooked. Baste from time to time. If the parsnips are to be served with meat which is not being roasted, they may be roasted by themselves in the oven in a mixture of butter and olive oil.

BAKED APPLE WITH YOGURT

1 lb Bramley apples
3 oz brown sugar
1½ oz butter
½ tsp cinnamon
yogurt

Peel, core and slice the apples. Place them in an ovenware dish. Cover them with soft brown sugar. Dot with nuts of butter and sprinkle with the cinnamon. Bake in a moderate oven until soft. Serve with yogurt.

CREAMED EGGS ON GARLIC TOAST

4 eggs
1 gill double cream
salt, pepper
1 clove garlic
2 oz butter
bread
fresh herbs

Butter a thick pan. Break the eggs into it and add the cream. Stir gently over a very low heat, blending well together. This very gentle cooking will probably take about 15 minutes, and the eggs should be stirred gently all the time. When cooked, season with salt, pepper and finely chopped fresh chives, parsley or tarragon. Rub a saucer with a cut clove of garlic. Cream the butter to a soft paste on this garlicky saucer. Toast some slices of bread, cut them into fancy shapes and spread them with the butter. Then pile them with the egg and serve either hot or cold.

POLPETTE

1 lb minced beef
2 eggs
3 garlic cloves
1 slice bread
milk
parsley
salt, pepper
nutmeg
lemon peel
flour
oil for frying

Blend together the minced beef, crushed garlic, some finely chopped parsley and 1 tsp grated lemon rind. Remove the crusts from a thick slice of bread. Soak the bread in a little milk, and when well soaked, blend this into the meat mixture. Blend in the beaten eggs, salt, pepper and a pinch of grated nutmeg. With floured hands form the mixture into small, flat cakes, each about the size of a half-crown. Roll them in flour. Make a small dent in the top of each. Fry them in very hot oil, turning them occasionally, until cooked and golden all over.

SEPTEMBER SALAD

1 head celery
5–6 walnuts
2 eating apples
1 small onion
1 green pepper
3 heads chicory
½ lemon
½ pint mayonnaise
salt, pepper

Chop the celery quite finely, using only the very crisp, tender pieces. Add the chopped walnuts, peeled and chopped apple and sliced chicory. Cut the pepper into thin slices, discarding the seeds. Pour boiling water over the strips of pepper and allow to stand for 2–3 minutes, before rinsing in cold water. Add the drained pepper to the other vegetables. Season with salt, pepper and the juice of ½ lemon. Toss well, then fold in the mayonnaise.

HOT FRUIT SALAD

2–3 tins of different fruits, such as mangoes, pineapple, lychees, black cherries, logan-berries, guavas, etc.

This is a perfect emergency pudding, though there is absolutely no reason why it should be reserved solely for emergencies. Just empty the tins of fruit into a pan, and heat them through. Serve with pouring cream.

CREAM OF CHICKEN SOUP

3 pints chicken stock
2 eggs
½ lemon
nutmeg
salt, pepper
4 dess ground rice
1 gill milk
small pieces cooked
   chicken
parsley

Heat the stock. Blend together the milk and ground rice until absolutely smooth. Add this to the hot stock and allow to simmer for 20–25 minutes. Blend in the juice of ½ lemon, a pinch of grated nutmeg, salt and pepper. Beat the eggs. Blend a little of the hot soup into the beaten eggs, and whisk well. Return this to the pan and reheat gently without allowing to boil. Garnish with strips of cooked chicken and finely chopped parsley before serving.

ROTI DE PORC BOULANGERE

2 lb boneless roasting
   pork
1 lb cooking apples
3 lb potatoes
2 oz butter
salt, pepper

Peel the apples and potatoes, and cut them into large chips. Put the butter in the bottom of a large fireproof dish. Add the apples and potatoes. Place the seasoned pork on top. Cook in a hot oven for 30 minutes, then reduce the heat and continue to cook for a further 1½ hours, or until the meat is tender. Baste frequently during cooking, and cover with a lid or foil if the meat is becoming too brown.

TOMATOES IN CREAM SAUCE

8 large tomatoes
1 gill double cream
salt, pepper
1 oz flour
1 oz butter
1 tbs oil
1 tsp sugar
parsley

Cut the tomatoes into thick slices. Dip the tomatoes into a mixture of salt, pepper and sugar, Then coat them on both sides with flour. Heat together the oil and butter. When hot add the tomatoes and fry them quickly on both sides until golden. Transfer them to a serving dish. Add the cream to the floury juices in the pan. Season with salt and pepper and stir well over a gentle heat for 3–4 minutes. Pour this sauce over the tomatoes and sprinkle with finely chopped parsley before serving.

LEMON WHIP

3 eggs
1 dess powdered gelatine
5 oz castor sugar
2 lemons

Separate the eggs. Whisk together the yolks and sugar until creamy. Soak the gelatine in 1 tbs cold water. Finely grate the rind of 1 lemon. Add this, together with 5 tbs strained lemon juice to the creamed egg yolk and sugar mixture. Pour 2 tbs hot water over the soaked gelatine and stir it well until the gelatine has dissolved completely. Add this to the gelatine mixture and stir well. Fold in the stiffly beaten egg whites, making sure that no streaks of white remain. Chill before serving.

DRESSED CRAB WITH AVOCADO

2 large avocados
½ tbs lemon juice
3 large tomatoes
2 tbs French dressing
lettuce
½ lb crab meat
mayonnaise

Quarter the avocados lengthwise, and peel them carefully. Sprinkle them with lemon juice. Halve the skinned tomatoes, discard the pips, and chop the tomato pulp finely. Toss it in 1 tbs French dressing. Just before serving shred some lettuce leaves finely, toss them in dressing and arrange them over the surface of a large serving plate. Arrange the avocados on top, filling their cavities with the tomato mixture. Pile the crab meat in the centre, and serve with mayonnaise.

NAVARIN PRINTANIER

3 lb diced lean lamb
2½ oz butter
3 small onions
2 oz flour
1 pint brown stock
salt, pepper
rosemary
1 clove garlic
1 bay leaf
1 lb new potatoes
½ lb new carrots
3–4 baby turnips
1½ lb fresh peas

Heat the butter in a large pan. Add the sliced onions and cook until they are golden and tender. Add the diced lamb. Toss well, until each piece is golden all over. Remove the pieces of meat and onions. To the butter in the pan add the flour. Stir well until light brown in colour, then gradually add the boiling stock, stirring all the time. When the sauce is blended, return the meat and onions to it. Season with salt, pepper, the crushed garlic, a few spikes of rosemary and a bay leaf. Cover with a lid and allow to simmer for 1 hour. Add the peeled potatoes, whole if tiny, and the peeled diced carrots and turnips. Cook gently for a further 40 minutes, then add the shelled peas. Cook until the peas are tender, by which time the navarin is ready. More stock may be needed during cooking.

PARSLIED RICE

½ lb Italian rice
6 tbs finely chopped
    parsley
2 tbs finely chopped
    chives
1 oz butter
½ gill single cream

Boil the rice in plenty of salted water for 12 minutes. Drain it well, then blend in the butter. In an ovenware dish place a layer of rice. Cover it with a layer of parsley and a sprinkling of chives. Repeat these layers of rice, parsley and chives until all the ingredients are used up. Pour the cream over and bake in a moderate oven for 10 minutes.

APPLE FOOL

1 lb Bramley apples
4 oz sugar
2 cloves
1 lemon
cinnamon
½ pint whipped cream

Peel, core and slice the apples. Cook them in a very little water, together with the cloves, a pinch of ground cinnamon and the peel of the lemon. When the apples are soft discard the cloves and peel. Drain off any surplus juice, reserving it for fruit salads or jellies. Liquidize the apples, or press them through a nylon sieve with a wooden spoon. To the resulting purée add the sugar and juice of 1 lemon. Stir well and allow to cool. Fold in the stiffly whipped cream and chill well.

CRUDITES WITH GARLIC MAYONNAISE

½ pint mayonnaise
1 large clove garlic
raw vegetables, such as:
carrots, cauliflower,
radishes, celery,
watercress, cucumber,
tomatoes, mushrooms

For this dish, you serve a pretty and nourishing selection of raw vegetables, washed and cut into convenient pieces. These are dipped— with fingers or forks— into mayonnaise, previously mixed with the crushed garlic.

CHICKEN SAUTE ARCHIDUC

1–3½ lb roasting chicken
flour
2 oz butter
½ gill sherry or white wine
1 tbs brandy
1 gill basic white sauce
½ gill single cream
salt, pepper

Cut the chicken into 8 pieces. Dust them with flour, salt and pepper. Heat the butter in a thick sauté pan. Add the chicken pieces and cook them gently for 20–25 minutes, covered with a lid. The chicken pieces will need turning frequently during cooking. When cooked, transfer them to a serving dish and keep them warm while preparing the sauce. To the juices in the pan add the sherry or white wine and the brandy. Allow to boil for 5 minutes. Blend in the white sauce and cream. Bring to the boil and allow to simmer for 5 minutes. Check the seasoning and pour the sauce over the chicken before serving.

COURGETTES AND ONIONS

1½ lb courgettes
2 large onions
salt, pepper
½ gill vermouth
2 oz butter

Heat the butter in a thick pan. Add the peeled and sliced onions and allow to cook gently for 3–4 minutes. Then add the courgettes, sliced but not peeled. Toss for a few minutes, then season with salt and pepper, and pour in the vermouth. Cover the pan and allow to cook gently for 10–15 minutes, or until the vegetables are tender.

BISCUIT CAKE

3 oz butter
3 oz castor sugar
5 tbs strong fresh coffee
½ lb digestive biscuits
1 egg
2 plain chocolate flake
   bars

Make some strong, fresh coffee. Crush the biscuits in a liquidizer, or wrapped in a tea towel and crushed with a rolling pin. Pour the coffee over the biscuit crumbs and stir well to make a moist crumb mixture. Cream together the butter and sugar. Gradually blend in the beaten egg yolk, and beat for 5 minutes. Add the stiffly beaten egg white, and mix well. Crumble one of the flake bars into the bottom of a sandwich cake tin. Then fill up the tin with alternate layers of biscuit and butter cream. Cover the top surface with the second flake bar, crumbled. Cover the tin with foil and chill for at least 6 hours. Loosen the edges before turning the cake out on to a serving plate.

GERMINY SOUP

½ lb sorrel
1 oz butter
½ oz sugar
3 pints chicken stock
4 egg yolks
1 gill single cream
salt, pepper

Wash and shake the sorrel, and shred it finely. Heat the butter in a thick pan, and add the shredded sorrel. Stir it for 2–3 minutes, then add the sugar, salt and pepper. Stir again, then add the boiling stock. Allow to simmer for 10 minutes. Whisk together the egg yolks and cream in the soup tureen. Slowly add the hot, but not boiling soup, whisking all the time. Check the seasoning before serving.

VEAL FLAMBE

4 veal cutlets
2 oz butter
½ lb mushrooms
2 tbs chopped parsley
1 tsp tarragon
2 tbs gin
1 gill chicken stock
1 gill double cream

Heat the butter in a thick frying pan. Fry the cutlets on both sides until golden, then season them with salt and pepper. Add the sliced mushrooms, parsley, tarragon and fry gently for 7–8 minutes. Warm the gin, pour it into the pan and set it alight. When the flames have subsided, transfer the meat and mushrooms to a serving dish and keep them warm. Stir the stock into the gin and juices in the frying pan. Bring to the boil, stirring well, then add the cream. Heat gently, without allowing to boil. Check the seasoning before pouring this over the veal and mushrooms.

BEANS WITH CELERY

½ lb haricot beans
4 oz butter
1 tbs lemon juice
1 gill double cream
nutmeg
2 stalks celery
salt, pepper

Soak the beans in cold water for 4 hours. Drain them. Put them in a pan with sufficient cold water to barely cover. Add 2 oz butter, a good sprinkling of freshly ground black pepper, and a trace of grated nutmeg. Bring to the boil and allow to simmer, uncovered, until the beans are almost cooked. Season with plenty of coarse salt, and continue to simmer until the beans are quite soft. Most of the liquid should have evaporated by this stage; if not, drain some of it away. Pour the cream over the beans, stir well and allow to cook for 5 minutes, then blend in the lemon juice. Cut the celery into thin, slanting strips. Fry them in the remaining butter until lightly browned. Transfer the cooked beans and sauce to a serving dish and top with the celery just before serving.

APPLE AND BLACKCURRANT MIROTON

2 oz butter
1 lb Bramley apples
½ lb blackcurrants
2–3 oz sugar
1 lemon

Melt the butter in a saucepan. Peel, core and slice the apples. Add them to the butter, together with the stalked blackcurrants. Cook gently until soft, stirring occasionally to prevent sticking. The fruit should be soft enough to form a soft pulp. When cooked, but still hot, sweeten it to taste, and stir in the grated rind of 1 lemon. Serve either hot or cold, with cream.

CREAM CHEESE WITH CRISPIES

8 oz best cream cheese
1 oz walnuts
1 small onion
4 inch cucumber
6 radishes
2 sticks celery
salt, pepper
1 tsp paprika

Finely chop the walnuts, peeled onion, cucumber, radishes and celery. Blend these crisp vegetables into the cream cheese. Season with salt, pepper and paprika. Serve on fingers of hot toast or slices of fresh French bread.

BEEF AND ONION GOULASH

1½ lb chuck steak
1½ lb onions
1 tbs paprika
1 tbs tomato purée
salt, pepper
1 tsp vinegar
1 tsp caraway seeds
marjoram
3 oz butter

Dice the beef, discarding any fat or gristle. Peel and slice the onions. Heat the butter in a thick pan. Add the onions and cook until golden brown. Stir in the paprika, then add 2 tbs cold water. Add the meat, and stir over the heat until the water has evaporated. Blend in the tomato purée, 1 tsp salt, freshly ground black pepper, the vinegar, caraway seeds and a pinch of marjoram. Cover the pan with a lid and allow to simmer very gently until the meat is tender, adding a little water from time to time, if necessary. When the meat is tender add another tablespoonful of water, stir well and cook quickly for a few more minutes.

CUCUMBER AND CHIVE SALAD

1 cucumber
1 gill cream
1 tsp castor sugar
1 tsp vinegar
2 tbs olive oil
salt, pepper
chives

Peel the cucumber and slice it very thinly. Sprinkle it with coarse salt in a colander. Cover it with a saucer and a heavy weight and allow it to drain for 1 hour. Squeeze out any remaining moisture. Blend together the sugar and vinegar. Add the cream, salt and pepper. Blend in the oil and about 2 tbs finely chopped chives. Pour this dressing over the cucumber before serving.

LEMON CAKE

2 lemons
4 oz unsalted butter
6 oz castor sugar
4 eggs
½ pint double cream
trifle sponges

Cream together the butter and sugar until light and fluffy. Beat in the egg yolks one at a time, ignoring the curdled effect which might occur. Add the grated rind and strained juice of the lemons. Fold in the stiffly beaten egg whites. Slice the sponge cakes through laterally three times. Fill a serving dish with alternate layers of sponge and lemon mixture. Chill overnight. Top with a layer of whipped cream and decorate with glacé cherries and flaked almonds.

BRESSANE MUSHROOM SOUP

2 oz butter
¾ lb mushrooms
1 clove garlic
parsley
salt, pepper
nutmeg
1 slice bread
1½ pints chicken stock

Heat the butter in a thick pan. Add the chopped mushrooms, crushed garlic, finely chopped parsley, salt, pepper and a pinch of nutmeg. Allow to seethe for a few minutes, Remove the crusts from the slice of bread. Soak the bread in a little of the boiling stock, for a few minutes. Stir this into the mushrooms, until well amalgamated. Add the remaining stock. Allow to simmer for 15 minutes. Liquidize, or rub the mixture through a sieve.

ESCALOPES DE VEAU A LA CREME

4 veal escalopes
1½ oz butter
salt, pepper
1 gill double cream

Season the escalopes with salt and pepper. Heat the butter in a thick frying pan. When hot, add the veal and cook gently, turning from time to time. When cooked, after about 8 minutes, transfer the escalopes to a warm serving dish and keep them hot. To the juices in the pan add the boiling cream. Stir well over a low flame for a few minutes, then pour this sauce over the veal before serving. This is a very delicately flavoured dish, and would be best served with plainly boiled new potatoes or a fine potato purée. Any salad or strongly flavoured vegetable should be served as a separate course, after the veal and its delicious sauce have disappeared.

LEMON LEEKS

2 lb leeks
salt, pepper
2 oz butter
1 lemon

Wash and trim the leeks. Using only the white parts, cut them into slices. Heat the butter in a thick pan. Add the sliced leeks, salt, pepper and the juice of 1 lemon. Allow to simmer gently for 15–20 minutes.

MINCEMEAT CRUMBLE

1 lb mincemeat
1 tbs brandy
3 oz butter
3 oz sugar
2 oz ground almonds
3 oz flour

Stir the brandy into the mincemeat and place it in the bottom of an ovenware dish. Rub together the butter, sugar, flour and ground almonds until of a fine crumb consistency. Cover the mincemeat with this and bake in a moderate oven for 1 hour. Serve hot, with pouring cream.

AUBERGINE FRITTERS

3 large aubergines
salt
4 oz flour
3 tbs olive oil
salt
1 egg white
oil for frying
1 lemon

Cut each aubergine in half, then into thin slices. Put them in a colander, sprinkle them with salt and leave to drain for an hour. Sieve the flour into a basin. Add a pinch of salt, and gradually stir in the oil and about 1 gill warm water. This batter should be of a cream consistency. Allow it to stand for at least 2 hours, then fold in the stiffly beaten egg white. Dip the drained aubergine slices in this batter before frying them in deep, very hot oil. When crisp and golden, drain them well and serve with lemon quarters.

IRISH STEW

8 best end neck cutlets
   of lamb
8 medium potatoes
1 large onion
1 medium carrot
1 tbs chopped parsley
salt, pepper

Trim the chops and place them round the inside edge of a saucepan. In the centre put the sliced carrot and onion, and the whole, peeled potatoes. Season to taste and cover with cold water. Bring to the boil and allow to cook gently for 1½ hours. Add the parsley, finely chopped and cook for a further 5 minutes.

SWEETCORN WITH HERB BUTTER

4 cobs sweetcorn
salt, pepper
4 oz butter
1 tbs finely chopped
   parsley
1 tbs finely chopped
   chives
1 tbs finely chopped
   tarragon
1 tsp sugar

Discard the husks and silk from the corns, and trim away any unripened tips. Bring to the boil a large panful of water. Add the sugar and corn. Bring back to the boil, and allow to cook for 8–10 minutes. Soften the butter slightly. Blend in salt, pepper and the chopped herbs. Serve this herb butter with the hot, drained sweetcorn.

GOOSEBERRY FOOL

1 lb gooseberries
4 oz sugar
1 gill double cream

Put the gooseberries and sugar in a pan, without topping and tailing them. Steam them until quite soft, then sieve them. Allow to cool, then blend in the whipped cream. Chill before serving.

FRENCH BEAN AND PRAWN SALAD

¾ lb French beans
6 oz peeled prawns or
   shrimps
3 tbs olive oil
1 tbs lemon juice
salt, pepper
2 eggs

Boil the French beans in very little salted water, but take care not to overcook them. They should still be a little crunchy. Blend together the oil and lemon juice. Drain the cooked beans and toss them in half the oil and lemon. Season with salt and pepper. Toss the prawns in the remaining oil and lemon and pile them on top of the beans. Hardboil the eggs. Shell them under cold, running water and cut them into quarters. Garnish the salad with these before serving.

VEAL PAPRIKA

4 veal escalopes
1 tbs oil
1 oz butter
1 tsp paprika
1 tbs flour
2 bay leaves
1 lemon
salt, pepper
½ pint double cream

Heat together the butter and oil in a thick frying pan. Sift together the flour, paprika, salt and pepper in a paper or plastic bag. Toss the escalopes in this, to coat them thoroughly without making any mess. Cook them, on one side only, in the hot oil and butter. Remove the meat from the pan and keep it warm. Drain off any surplus fat from the pan, and to the remaining juices add the bay leaves, the thinly pared rind of ½ lemon and 1 tbs lemon juice. Stir well, then return the escalopes to this sauce, cooked sides uppermost. Cover with a lid and cook gently for 20 minutes. Transfer the meat to a serving plate, and keep it warm, while boiling the sauce quickly to reduce it well. Gradually stir in the cream, and reheat gently without allowing to boil. Pour this sauce over the veal and garnish with lemon quarters and sprigs of watercress.

PURPLE BROCCOLI WITH LEMON BUTTER

1½ lb broccoli
salt, pepper
3 oz butter
½ lemon

Wash the broccoli, discarding any large leaves and tough stalks. Place the broccoli in deep, boiling salted water and cook fairly quickly for 20 minutes. Drain it well. To the butter add the grated rind and juice of ½ lemon. Heat this gently and pour it over the broccoli before serving.

PEAR FOOL

4 large ripe pears
2 oz castor sugar
1 lemon
ground ginger
1½ gills double cream

Peel, core and slice the pears. Boil together the sugar, 1 gill water, a pinch of ground ginger and the juice of 1 lemon. When this is of a syrup consistency, add the sliced pears and poach them until tender. Strain off the juice, using it for fruit salad, jellies, etc. Purée the pears. Allow to cool. Blend in the whipped cream, and chill before serving.

ONIONS WITH VINAIGRETTE SAUCE

4 large onions
6 tbs oil
2 tbs wine vinegar
salt, pepper
½ tsp French mustard
parsley

Do not peel the onions, but place them, whole, on a baking sheet and cook in a low oven for 2–2¼ hours, or until tender. Allow to cool. Peel and arrange them in a serving dish. Whisk together the oil, vinegar, salt, pepper and mustard. Pour this over the onions and garnish with finely chopped parsley before serving.

CALF'S KIDNEYS IN VODKA

2 calf's kidneys
1 oz butter
2 tbs vodka
4 oz mushrooms
1 slice boiled ham
2 tbs double cream
salt, pepper
nutmeg
parsley

Cut the kidneys into small pieces, discarding any fat or gristle. Heat ½ oz butter in a pan. Add the kidneys and 1 tbs vodka and allow to cook gently. Meanwhile, heat the remaining butter in a second pan, and gently fry the chopped mushrooms and ham. Pour in the remaining vodka. Allow to cook for 2 minutes. Stir in the cream and allow the sauce to reduce for a few minutes. Blend in the cooked kidneys. Season with salt, pepper and a pinch of nutmeg. Sprinkle with finely chopped parsley before serving.

MARROW IN BUTTER

1 medium vegetable
  marrow
2 oz butter
salt, pepper
fresh dill

Peel the marrow and cut it into bite-size slices. Arrange them in a buttered ovenware dish. Cover with nuts of butter. Season with salt and pepper and sprigs of dill. Cook in a moderate oven until tender, basting frequently.

CHESTNUT SNOW

10 oz tinned sweetened
  chestnut purée
½ pint double cream
4 egg whites
½ lemon

Stir the lemon juice into the chestnut purée. Whisk the egg whites until stiff. In a separate bowl whisk the cream until stiff. Fold the egg whites into the cream gradually, then mix in the chestnut purée. Serve chilled.

MUSHROOM SOUP

1 small onion
½ lb mushrooms
1 oz butter
1 oz flour
1 pint milk
2 tbs double cream
salt, pepper

Melt the butter in a thick pan. Add the chopped, peeled onion, and fry gently until golden. Add the chopped mushrooms, stir well and cook for 1 minute only. Sprinkle in the flour. Gradually add the boiling milk, stirring all the time. Season to taste, and allow to simmer for 8 minutes. Just before serving, reheat and blend in the cream and a knob of butter.

CASSEROLE DE BOEUF DAUPHINOISE

4 thin steaks (sirloin or rump)
2 large onions
3 tbs oil
1 tbs vinegar
2 tbs finely chopped parsley
2 cloves garlic
1 oz flour
salt, pepper
4 anchovy fillets
1 oz butter

Heat the butter in a frying pan. Season the steaks and fry them quickly on both sides until brown. Peel and slice the onions and fry them in butter, too. Arrange half the onions in the bottom of an ovenware dish, cover with the steaks, then the remaining onions. Blend together the oil, vinegar, chopped parsley, crushed garlic, flour, salt, pepper and anchovy fillets, pounded to a paste. Cover the onion with this mixture and cook, tightly covered, in a moderate oven for 30 minutes.

RICE WITH ALMONDS AND RAISINS

½ lb Italian rice
1 large onion
2 tbs oil
2 tbs raisins
2 oz flaked almonds
salt, pepper
½ oz butter

Heat the oil in a thick pan. Fry the sliced onion until golden. Add the rice and stir for a few minutes. Pour in sufficient boiling stock or water to cover. Season with salt and pepper and allow to simmer gently for 10 minutes, or until the rice is almost cooked. Blend in the raisins and almonds and continue to cook until the rice is soft. Drain and serve topped with a nut of butter.

GRAPEFRUIT CREAM

2 grapefruit
1 orange
3 oz castor sugar
1 pint double cream
sponge cake

In the bottom of a serving dish place a layer of sponge cake, or trifle sponges. Grate the rind of 1 orange and 1 grapefruit. *Add the juice of 1 orange and 2 grapefruit. Sweeten to taste. Blend in the cream, stirring well. Pour the grapefruit cream over the sponge cake and allow to stand in a cool place for at least 3 hours before serving.

*If possible use a squeezer on a handle, rather than one with a strainer, as the tiny grapefruit 'tears' add an interesting texture to the cream.

BAKED MUSHROOMS

½ lb button mushrooms
2½ oz butter
salt, pepper
3 oz fresh breadcrumbs
1 tbs finely chopped parsley
1 tbs finely chopped chives
1 oz grated parmesan cheese

Use ½ oz butter to grease a shallow ovenproof dish. Take the small, whole mushrooms. Wipe, but do not wash or peel them. Arrange them, stalks uppermost, in the dish. Season well with salt and pepper. Mix together the breadcrumbs, parsley, chives and cheese. Sprinkle this over the mushrooms. Heat the remaining butter until melted. Pour it over the breadcrumbs. Bake in a moderate oven for 10–15 minutes.

MEXICAN CHICKEN CASSEROLE

1 roasting chicken
2 large onions
2 cloves garlic
1 tbs flour
2 tbs tomato purée
4 cloves
1 tbs vinegar
1 cupful sherry
1 large green pepper
12 stoned black olives
½ cupful seeded raisins
3 tbs oil
salt, pepper

Heat the oil in a frying pan. Joint the chicken. Fry the chicken pieces quickly in hot oil until golden brown all over. Transfer them to a large casserole dish. Peel and slice the onions and fry them together with the chopped garlic, until golden. Sprinkle in the flour, stir well and cook for a few moments over a gentle heat, then pour in the tomato purée and 1 cupful water. Stir well, bring to the boil, then pour this over the chicken. Add the cloves, vinegar, sherry, sliced green pepper, salt and pepper. Cover with a lid and cook in a moderate oven for 1 hour. Add the olives and raisins and cook for a further 15 minutes.

SPAGHETTI WITH GREEN BUTTER

½ lb spaghetti
salt, pepper
3 oz unsalted butter
1 tbs finely chopped chives
2 tbs finely chopped parsley
1 tbs finely chopped thyme

Have ready a large pan of boiling salted water. Add the spaghetti, coiling it round the pan as it softens. Allow to boil for 11–12 minutes, then drain it well. Soften the butter slightly. Season it with salt and pepper. Blend in the herbs and mix well. Add this butter to the spaghetti just before serving and toss it well, to make sure that each strand of spaghetti glistens with savoury butter.

HAWAIIAN ICE

3 ripe bananas
⅛ pint fresh orange juice
⅛ pint milk
⅛ pint crushed pineapple
2 oz macaroons, crumbled
5 oz sugar
3 tbs lemon juice
½ pint double cream

Peel and mash the bananas. Bring the milk to the boil, then allow it to cool. Whip the cream. Blend together all the ingredients. Place them in an ice-making tray, cover with foil and freeze at maximum temperature for 2½ hours, agitating with a fork twice during freezing.

TOMATO SOUP

½ oz butter
3 oz bacon
1 medium onion
½ lb tomatoes
¾ pint beef stock
1 oz cornflour

Melt the butter in a thick pan. Add the diced, rindless bacon, skinned, chopped tomatoes, and chopped onion. Stir well, and add the boiling stock. Allow to simmer for a few minutes, until the tomatoes are absolutely soft. Liquidize, or rub the mixture through a sieve. Stir a little of the hot soup into the cornflour, and mix to a smooth paste, then add this to the remaining soup, stirring well. Cook gently for a further 2 minutes. Check the seasoning. Sprinkle with finely chopped fresh herbs before serving.

LAMB CASSEROLE WITH CHESTNUTS

2 lb lean lamb
2 lb chestnuts
1 large onion
2 oz butter
1 tbs flour
½ pint chicken stock
1 tbs sugar
salt, pepper

Score the chestnuts with the point of a sharp knife. Bake them in the oven until the outer shells and inside skins may be peeled off easily. Heat the butter in a thick pan. Add the sliced onion and cook until golden brown. Add the lamb, cut into small cubes. Toss until all the meat is well seared and brown all over. Sprinkle in the flour and stir well over a gentle heat for a few minutes. Gradually stir in the hot stock, salt and pepper. Cover the pan with a lid and allow to simmer gently for 30 minutes. Add the chestnuts, and allow to cook for a further 1 hour, after which time the meat and chestnuts should be quite tender. Stir in the sugar just before serving.

CABBAGE WITH NUTMEG

1 medium cabbage
1 medium onion
salt, pepper
2 oz butter
nutmeg
2–3 tbs stock

Heat the butter in a thick pan. Add the peeled and sliced onion and allow to cook for 3–4 minutes, then add the shredded cabbage. Stir over the heat for 5 minutes. Season with salt, pepper and a good sprinkling of freshly grated nutmeg. Stir well. Add the stock, cover the pan and allow to cook for a further 10 minutes. Add another sprinkling of nutmeg just before serving.

ITALIAN SYLLABUB

½ pint double cream
1 gill sweet vermouth
4 oz castor sugar
1 lemon

Grate the rind of the lemon. Squeeze and strain the juice of the lemon. Whisk together the cream, lemon rind, lemon juice, sugar and vermouth until thick. Put it into tall serving glasses and chill for at least 3 hours before serving. Sponge fingers or almond shortbread biscuits go well with this rich sweet.

JAMBON AUX OEUFS

4 slices boiled ham
4 eggs
4 tbs double cream
1½ oz butter
salt, pepper

Heat 1 oz butter in a frying pan. Break in the eggs very carefully and season with salt and pepper. Fry gently until almost set, then pour the cream over each egg and allow to cook for a further 2 minutes. Meanwhile heat the remaining butter in a second pan. Add the slices of ham and turn them over and over in this butter until warmed through. Top each slice of ham with a creamy egg before serving.

FILLET STEAKS, SAUCE BELGE

4 fillet steaks
2 oz butter
salt, pepper
1 tbs mixed English
   mustard
1 tbs French mustard
4 tbs double cream

Heat 1 oz butter in a thick frying pan. Cook the seasoned steaks in this, on both sides, in the usual way. When cooked, transfer the steaks to a warmed plate, and keep them hot. Add the remaining butter to the juices in the pan, and when melted, stir in the two mustards and the cream. Stir well and when hot and well blended, pour this over the steaks.

ISRAELI SALAD

1 small lettuce
2 eggs
½ green pepper
2 tomatoes
1 inch cucumber
4 large spring onions
2 tbs olive oil
½ lemon

Wash the lettuce and tear the leaves into small pieces. Soft boil the eggs. Slice the green pepper finely, pour boiling water over it, allow to stand for 2 minutes, then run cold water over it. Peel and roughly chop the tomatoes. Cut the cucumber and spring onions into small pieces. Blend together the lettuce, pepper, tomatoes, cucumber and spring onions. Roughly chop the eggs and add them to the other ingredients. Pour over the juice of ½ lemon, then the oil. Mix well, but gently, so that the egg yolk blends itself into the oil and lemon.

STRAWBERRY CREME BRULEE

1 lb strawberries or
   raspberries
1 tbs castor sugar
2 tbs brandy or Cointreau
½ pint double cream
6 oz demerara sugar

Hull the strawberries or raspberries (or a mixture of both fruit). Arrange them in an ovenware soufflé dish, and sprinkle them with the castor sugar and brandy. Whip the cream until stiff. Cover the strawberries with this and allow to stand in the refrigerator overnight. Spread the demerara sugar over the cream, in a layer at least ½ inch thick. Pop under the grill for a few minutes, until the sugar caramelizes. Serve at once.

TUNA FISH PATE

6-oz tin tuna fish
3 oz unsalted butter
pepper
lemon juice

Cream the tuna fish in a liquidizer or mortar. Work in the softened butter. When quite smooth, season with a few drops of lemon juice and some freshly milled black pepper. Put the mixture in a pot and serve very cold, garnished with finely chopped chives or capers. Serve with hot fingers of toast or crusty French bread.

WINE BAKED VEAL

1½ lb lean veal
3 oz butter
1 tbs flour
1½ cupfuls milk
2 tbs sliced green pepper
½ gill white wine or
   vermouth

Trim the meat of any fat or sinews. Cut the meat into 1-inch cubes. Heat the butter in a heavy frying pan. Cook the meat in the butter, with a lid on, for 20 minutes over a moderate heat. Remove the lid, increase the heat and continue to cook until the veal is lightly browned all over. Sprinkle in the flour and stir well. Gradually add the warm milk, stirring all the time, and cook until the sauce is smooth. Blend in the green pepper, salt and pepper. Transfer the mixture to a buttered ovenware dish and cook, covered, for 45 minutes. Blend in the wine, and cook for a further 10 minutes.

LEEKS AND TOMATOES

1½ lb leeks
salt, pepper
½ lemon
4–5 large tomatoes
2 oz butter

Wash and trim the leeks. Using only the white parts, cut the leeks into slices. Heat the butter in a thick pan. Add the leeks, salt, pepper, juice of ½ lemon and the tomatoes, peeled and quartered. Allow to simmer gently for 15 minutes. The tomatoes should provide enough liquid to prevent burning; if not, add a little stock or water.

STUFFED PEACHES

4 large yellow peaches
3 oz almond macaroons
1 egg yolk
1 oz butter
2 oz castor sugar

Halve and stone the peaches. Remove a little of the peach flesh, to make a good-sized hollow. Crumble the macaroons finely. Add the peach flesh, egg yolk, butter and sugar. Mix well and stuff each peach half with a little of this mixture. Bake them in a buttered ovenware dish for 30 minutes. Serve either hot or cold, with pouring cream.

SWEETCORN WITH BUTTER

4 cobs sweetcorn
4 oz unsalted butter
salt, pepper
paprika
1 tbs finely chopped
  chives
1 tbs finely chopped
  parsley
1 tbs finely chopped
  mint

Trim the sweetcorn of husks and silk. Place the cobs in a pan of unsalted water, bring back to the boil and allow to simmer gently for 15–20 minutes. Meanwhile, cream the butter with a fork. Season it with salt, pepper, 1 tsp paprika and the finely chopped herbs. Mix well. Drain the cooked corn, and top each serving with a portion of herb butter.

STROGOULASH

1½ lb fillet steak
1 oz butter
1 tbs oil
1 tsp salt
1 tbs paprika
1 oz flour
4 large onions
4 large potatoes
½ pint red wine
1½ cupfuls sour cream
beef or chicken stock

This dish is halfway between a goulash and a stroganoff—hence its name. Cut the steak into large, thick matchsticks, as for Stroganoff. Heat the butter and oil together in a thick pan. Add the steak, salt, paprika, sliced onions and sliced potatoes. Sprinkle in the flour and stir well. Allow to cook until lightly browned, then add the wine, 1 cupful sour cream and sufficient stock to barely cover. Transfer to a casserole, cover with a lid and cook in a moderate oven for 1 hour. Just before serving, blend in the remaining sour cream.

TOMATES PROVENCALES EN SALADE

6 large tomatoes
2 cloves garlic
olive oil
salt, pepper
parsley

Slice the tops off the tomatoes. Soften the pulp with a teaspoon. Sprinkle the tomatoes with salt and allow them to drain, upside down, in a colander. Meanwhile, pound together 2 garlic cloves, 2 tbs olive oil, 2 tbs finely chopped parsley and a large pinch of salt. Fill the drained tomatoes with this mixture and allow to stand for 2 hours before serving.

MARMINCE PIE

½ lb short pastry
¾ lb mincemeat
4 tbs chunky marmalade
icing sugar
whipped cream

Blend together the mincemeat and marmalade, adding a dash of brandy, if liked. Make a mince pie, or small mince tarts, in the usual way using the 'marmince' mixture. Bake them as usual. Sprinkle with icing sugar and serve hot, with dollops of whipped cream.

CURRIED PARSNIP SOUP

1 medium parsnip
1 medium onion
3 oz butter
1 clove garlic
1 tbs flour
1 tsp curry powder
2 pints beef stock
1 gill cream

Peel and chop the onion and parsnip. Heat the butter in a thick pan. Add the crushed clove of garlic and chopped vegetables. Cover and allow to cook gently for 10 minutes. Stir in the flour and curry powder, and gradually add the boiling stock. Allow to simmer gently until the parsnip is tender, about 15 minutes. Liquidize, or rub the mixture through a sieve. Check the seasoning, and stir in the cream just before serving.

FRICANDEAU OF VEAL

1½ lb veal fillet
½ lb bacon rashers
½ pint stock
1 tbs potato flour
2 carrots
2 small onions
thyme, parsley
3 cloves
salt, pepper

Peel and slice the carrots and onions. Place them in the bottom of an ovenware casserole, together with a sprig of thyme and parsley, the cloves, salt, pepper and 3–4 bacon rashers cut into squares. Wrap the veal in the remaining bacon rashers, and arrange it on top of the vegetables. Pour over the boiling stock. Cook, uncovered, in a moderate oven for 1½ hours, basting from time to time. Transfer the veal to a plate and keep it warm while thickening the sauce, by blending in the potato flour, previously mixed with a little cold water. Return the meat to the casserole dish, coat it with the sauce and cook for a further 5 minutes.

CASSEROLED SPRING GREENS

1½ lb spring greens
salt, pepper
1 gill milk
2 tbs double cream

Wash and pick over the spring greens, cutting them into suitable serving pieces. Boil them for 3 minutes in salted water then drain them well. Arrange them in an ovenware dish. Sprinkle with salt and pepper. Pour over the milk. Cover the casserole with foil and a lid, to ensure that no steam escapes, and bake in a moderate oven for 1 hour. Just before serving, pour over the cream.

APRICOT CRUSTS

1 lb apricots
4 thick slices wholemeal
  or granary bread
2 oz butter
2 oz brown sugar

Thickly butter each slice of bread. Halve the apricots and discard the stones. Arrange apricot halves all over each buttered bread slice, hollow sides uppermost. Sprinkle them with sugar and nuts of butter and bake, covered with a sheet of buttered greaseproof paper, for 30 minutes in a moderate oven. Serve with cream.

MARINADED KIPPERS

1 lb kipper fillets
1 large onion
2 tbs vinegar
6 tbs oil
pepper

Remove the skin from the kipper fillets. Place the fillets in a plastic container with an airtight lid. Add the finely sliced onion and plenty of freshly milled black pepper. Whisk together the oil and vinegar with a fork and pour this over the kippers. Cover with the lid and allow to stand in a cool place for 24 hours, turning the container over from time to time to ensure even marinading. Serve with thin slices of buttered granary bread.

STUFFED GREEN PEPPERS

4 large green peppers
½ lb minced beef and pork
2 oz rice
1 small onion
salt, pepper
parsley
1½ oz butter

for sauce:
1 lb tomatoes
1 oz butter
1 small onion
1 tbs flour
sugar
1 tbs lemon juice
salt, pepper

First make the sauce. Heat 1 oz butter in a thick pan. Add the peeled and sliced onion and cook gently until lightly brown. Add the sliced and peeled tomatoes, salt, pepper and a pinch of sugar. Cook until the tomatoes begin to soften, then stir in the flour. Add the lemon juice, cover barely level with water and allow to simmer for 10 minutes. Meanwhile, slice the tops off the peppers carefully. Scoop out and discard the seeds and membranes. Pour boiling water over the peppers and lids and allow to stand for 5 minutes, then drain well. Heat 1½ oz butter in a frying pan. Add the chopped onion and cook until golden. Stir in the rice and cook until it becomes transparent. Add 1 gill water and cook until the water has all been absorbed by the rice. Blend in the minced meat, salt, pepper and lots of finely chopped parsley. Stuff each pepper with this mixture, and top them with their lids. Stand them upright in a casserole, making sure that they will not fall over. Liquidize the sauce, or press it through a sieve, and pour it over the peppers. Cover the casserole with a lid, or foil, and bake in a low oven for about 1 hour.*

* This dish may be cooked on top of the stove, if that is more convenient.

MIXED SALAD

½ lettuce
2 pieces chicory
3 tomatoes
½ cucumber
2 stalks celery
watercress
1 clove garlic
6 tbs oil
2 tbs vinegar
salt, pepper
½ tsp French mustard

Rub a salad bowl with the cut garlic clove. Into it put the washed and shredded lettuce leaves, chicory cut into slices, peeled and diced cucumber, chopped celery and a few sprigs of watercress. Mix together the oil, vinegar, mustard, salt and pepper. Pour the dressing over the salad and toss thoroughly before serving.

STRAWBERRY FOOL

1 lb strawberries
3 oz sugar
1 gill double cream

Hull the strawberries, then press them through a nylon sieve, using a wooden spoon. Stir the sugar into the purée. Whip the cream. Gradually fold in the purée until no streaks of white remain. Chill well before serving.

MUSHROOM, CUCUMBER AND FRENCH BEAN SALAD

½ lb button mushrooms
½ lb French beans
½ cucumber
3 tbs oil
1 garlic clove
½ lemon
salt, pepper

Boil the beans in salted water in the usual way, taking care not to over-cook them. Drain them, and while they are still hot, toss them in 1 tablespoonful of oil and a little lemon juice. Arrange them in a serving dish. Slice the mushrooms. Add the diced, unpeeled cucumber. Season this mixture with salt, pepper, the crushed garlic, the remaining oil and lemon juice to taste. Mix well, and pile this mixture on top of the beans before serving, chilled.

ROAST STUFFED LEG OF LAMB

1 boned leg of lamb
2 tbs butter
1 gill stock or red wine

for stuffing:
3 rashers bacon
1 small onion
1 tsp chopped parsley
½ tsp thyme or rosemary
4 tbs breadcrumbs
4 tbs milk
½ lemon
salt, pepper

for sauce:
3 large onions
2 tbs butter
1 tbs flour
½ pint milk
nutmeg
½ gill cream
salt, pepper

First make the stuffing, by soaking the breadcrumbs in the milk. Then blend in all the other stuffing ingredients, finely chopped. Pack this mixture into the cavity left by the leg bone. Any surplus stuffing can be formed into small balls and placed around the joint during cooking. Season the lamb with plenty of freshly ground black pepper. Place it in a roasting tray, together with the butter. Bake in a moderate oven, allowing 20 minutes per pound. When cooked, strain the gravy into a saucepan, discarding any surplus fat. Boil up the gravy and stock or red wine quickly until well reduced. Meanwhile, slice the onions thinly. Melt the butter in a pan. Fry the onions gently until soft but not brown. Sprinkle in the flour, stir well, then gradually add the milk, stirring all the time. Season with nutmeg, salt and pepper. Just before serving, blend in the cream. Arrange the cooked leg of lamb on a serving plate, on a bed of watercress. Serve the onion sauce separately.

BAKED BEETROOT IN CREAM

4 medium raw beetroot
1 lemon
1½ gills double cream
salt, pepper
1 oz butter

Wash but do not peel the beetroot. Place each one on a sheet of buttered foil. Wrap them carefully, arrange on a baking tray and bake in a moderate oven for 1½–1¾ hours, or until tender. Peel and thinly slice them into a saucepan. Add the cream, salt, pepper and then heat gently. Just before serving, stir in the lemon juice.

RHUBARB CRUMBLE

1 lb rhubarb
3 oz sugar
1 gill water
4 oz butter
4 oz castor sugar
4 oz flour
2 oz ground almonds

Boil together the sugar and water, until of a syrup consistency. Add the cleaned rhubarb, cut into 1 inch lengths. Allow to cook for 5 minutes only, then drain it, reserving the juice for fruit salads, jellies, etc. Place the part-cooked rhubarb in the bottom of an ovenware dish. Rub together the flour, butter, sugar and ground almonds until of a crumb consistency. Cover the fruit with this mixture. Bake in a moderate oven for 1½ hours, covering with a lid or foil for the first hour. Serve with pouring cream or custard.

SPRING SOUP

1 medium onion
½ green pepper
2 medium carrots
1½ oz butter
6 large lettuce leaves
1¼ pint chicken stock
salt, pepper

Slice the onion, pepper and carrots very finely. Heat the butter in a thick pan, add the finely sliced vegetables and toss over a gentle flame for 5–10 minutes. Add the very finely shredded lettuce. Stir well for a few minutes. Add the boiling stock and allow to simmer for 10 minutes. Check the seasoning before serving.

BRAISED BEEF WITH PRUNES

2 lb chuck (or other
  good stewing) steak
1 large onion
1 tbs oil
1 clove garlic
salt, pepper
½ pint brown ale or stout
1 tbs flour
water
½ lb prunes
hazelnuts

Trim the meat and cut it into quite large pieces, not dice. Heat the oil. Fry the peeled and sliced onion until golden, then add the meat. Cook until brown on both sides, then sprinkle in the flour, stirring well. Pour over the beer, add the chopped garlic, salt and pepper and blend it all together well. If the sauce appears too thick blend in a little water. Transfer the mixture to an ovenware dish, cover it with a lid and allow to cook in a low oven for 2 hours. Meanwhile, soak and cook the prunes until they are soft enough to stone. Toast a handful of hazelnuts under the grill. Stuff each prune with one or two hazelnuts, and add them to the cooked beef. Cook for a further 30 minutes.

CASSEROLED POTATOES

2 lb potatoes
1 gill stock
2 oz butter
salt, pepper

Peel and thinly slice the potatoes. Allow them to soak in cold water for 10 minutes. Drain them well. Arrange them in a buttered ovenware dish, seasoning each layer well with salt and pepper. Add the stock, and the butter cut into pieces. Cook in a moderate oven for about 1 hour, after which time the potatoes should be tender, the liquid absorbed and the top lightly browned.

CHEESE WITH FRUIT

selection of cheeses
fruit

Serve your selection of cheeses with fruit. But not just apples and grapes. In the appropriate seasons, serve a bowl of black cherries, dessert gooseberries, slices of fresh pineapple, melon cubes, fresh lychees or figs.

PORTUGUESE SARDINES

2 large tins sardines
 packed in olive oil
1 large onion
3 large tomatoes
1 lemon
pepper
1 tbs finely chopped
 parsley
2–3 sprigs thyme
lettuce
watercress

Place the sardines and their oil in a flat serving dish. Cover with the thinly sliced onion and sliced, peeled tomatoes. Add the juice of 1 lemon, some freshly milled black pepper, the parsley and thyme. Allow to stand for at least 1 hour before serving on a bed of shredded lettuce and watercress.

ROAST GROUSE WITH WHITE GRAPES

2 young grouse
6 rashers fat bacon
1 gill port or sherry
salt, pepper
4 oz butter
½ lb seeded, peeled
 white grapes

Wrap each bird in bacon rashers, and put a large knob of butter inside each. Place them in a roasting pan and cook in a hot oven for 20 minutes. Pour over the port and continue cooking for a further 10 minutes, basting frequently. Transfer the cooked grouse to a hot serving dish. Cook the gravy over a high flame until well reduced, and serve this separately. Serve with a bowl of seeded, peeled white grapes which, prepared a short while in advance, will provide their own juice.

PEAS WITH CREAM

1 lb shelled peas
1 gill double cream
salt, pepper
castor sugar
mint

Cook the peas in boiling salted water for about 30 minutes, together with a sprig of mint. When the peas are tender but not mushy, drain them. Place them in a second pan, together with the cream, a pinch of sugar, salt and pepper. Reheat gently, without allowing to boil, and serve very hot.

CREAM CHEESE AND CHESTNUT

½ lb best cream cheese
2 tbs single cream
3 tbs tinned, sweetened
 chestnut purée
1 lemon
2 tbs finely chopped
 pistachio or almonds

Grate the rind of the lemon. Squeeze and strain the juice of ½ lemon. Blend together the lemon juice, rind, cream cheese, cream, chestnut purée and nuts. When well blended, chill lightly before serving with sponge fingers.

CARROT AND WATERCRESS SOUP

½ lb onions
1 oz butter
1 lb potatoes
1½ pints chicken stock
4 oz carrots
1 bunch watercress
1 gill single cream
salt, pepper

Peel and slice the onions. Heat the butter in a thick pan, add the onions and allow to cook gently until soft but not brown. Add the peeled and sliced potatoes and boiling stock. Bring to the boil again, cover and allow to simmer for about 30 minutes, by which time the potatoes should be soft. Liquidize, or press the mixture through a sieve. Check the seasoning. Just before serving, stir in the cream, the peeled, finely grated raw carrot and finely chopped watercress leaves. Serve either hot or cold.

SCALOPPINE PIZZAIUOLA

2 lb lean veal
3 green peppers
4 oz mushrooms
2 chilli peppers

for sauce:
2 cloves garlic
2 onions
1 large tin tomatoes
marjoram
oil

First make the sauce. Heat 4 dessertspoonfuls of oil in a very thick pan. When really hot add the crushed garlic. When brown add the thinly sliced onions. Allow to cook gently until soft, but not brown. Add the tomatoes and cook more quickly for 15 minutes. Add 1 dessertspoonful of fresh marjoram, or a large pinch of dried marjoram, and cook for a further 5 minutes. Heat 4 dessertspoonfuls of oil in a second, thick pan. Add the veal, cut into small slices. Gradually reduce the heat, and when the veal is lightly brown on both sides add the peppers, each cut into 8 long slices. Cover the pan and allow to cook very gently for 10 minutes, stirring from time to time. Add the sliced mushrooms and cook uncovered for 10 minutes. Pour in the tomato sauce and add the chilli peppers. Bring to a rapid boil. Cook for 10 minutes, then lower the heat for a final 5 minutes.

SWEDISH POTATOES

2 lb small new potatoes
3 large onions
1 gill cream
2 tbs vinegar
1 oz castor sugar
salt, pepper
2 oz butter

Boil the potatoes in salted water, without peeling them. Peel them while still hot, then allow to cool. Meanwhile, heat the butter in a pan. Add the peeled and thinly sliced onions and allow to simmer gently until cooked, adding a little water if necessary. Season with salt and pepper. Add the sugar, vinegar and cream. Blend in the potatoes. Mix well and reheat gently for 10–15 minutes. This dish may be served hot or cold.

GATEAU MALAKOFF

½ lb unsalted butter
4 oz raisins
2 tbs kirsch
½ lb castor sugar
½ lb ground almonds
2 tbs double cream
½ lb sponge fingers
8–10 pistachio nuts

Malakoff, like goulash and hotpot, is one of those dishes for which every family has its own favourite recipe. The flavours can be varied widely, according to your whims, but the result is a rich pudding without much culinary effort. Wipe, stone and halve the raisins. Soak them overnight in the kirsch. Soften the butter slightly and, with a fork, blend in the ground almonds, sugar and finely chopped pistachio nuts. Cream this mixture well for 10 minutes, then blend in the cream, kirsch and raisins. Butter a soufflé mould, or a cake tin with a removable base. Line the bottom of it with a pretty arrangement of sponge fingers, bearing in mind that this will be the top surface of the finished gâteau. Fill the mould with alternate layers of sponge fingers and almond mixture, ending with a layer of sponge fingers. Press down well, then allow to chill overnight. Turn out on to a serving plate, and serve with whipped cream, flavoured with a few drops of kirsch.

SWEET PEPPER AND OLIVE SALAD

1 green pepper
1 red pepper
1 small onion
salt
sugar
olive oil
lemon juice
2 oz black olives
1 small tin tuna fish

Cut the peppers into small fine strips, discarding any seeds. Wash them and pour boiling water over them. Allow to stand for 2 minutes, then rinse well in cold water. Transfer them to a serving dish. Peel the onion and cut it into tissue thin rounds. Add these to the peppers, sprinkle with a pinch of sugar and 2 tsp salt and allow to stand for an hour. Drain off some of the juices. Blend together 2 tbs olive oil and 1 tbs lemon juice or wine vinegar. Toss the pepper, onions and flaked tuna fish in this, before strewing with black olives and finely chopped parsley.

STEAK, KIDNEY AND MUSHROOMS

2 lb lean beef
½ lb diced kidney
2 large onions
1 clove garlic
1 oz flour
salt, pepper
1 bay leaf
ground mace
dry mustard
2 oz mushrooms
½ pint beef stock
1 glassful sherry
Worcester sauce

In a large paper or plastic bag put the flour, salt, pepper, a pinch of ground mace, a pinch of dry mustard and a crumbled, dried bay leaf. Dice the beef and kidney, discarding any fat or sinews. Toss the meat in the flour in the bag, then place it in an ovenware dish. Mix in the sliced onions, mushrooms and chopped garlic. Blend together the stock, sherry and a dash of Worcester sauce. Pour this over the meat and vegetables. Cover with a lid, and cook in a very low oven for 3½ hours.*

 * If required for a pie, allow the mixture to cool, skim off any surplus fat, then cover with a pastry lid and bake in fairly hot oven until golden.

JERUSALEM ARTICHOKES

2 lb Jerusalem artichokes
salt, pepper
2 oz butter
½ lemon

Choose artichokes of similar size, if possible. Cook them, in boiling salted water, without peeling them. They become soft quite quickly and will disintegrate if allowed to overcook. So test frequently with a skewer, and remove them from the pan as soon as they are cooked. Because of their irregular shapes, some may cook more quickly than others, so take care to test them all. When cooked, drain them and as soon as they are cool enough to handle, peel them. Heat the butter, salt, pepper and the juice of ½ lemon in a pan. Add the artichokes, and toss in this for 5 minutes before serving.

POTS AU CHOCOLAT

4 eggs
½ gill double cream
2½ oz icing sugar
1 dess brandy
4 oz rich dark chocolate

Separate the eggs. Place the yolks, melted chocolate, cream and icing sugar in the liquidizer. Liquidize at the highest speed for 3 minutes. Add the unbeaten egg whites and brandy and liquidize for a further 3 minutes. Transfer to individual cocotte dishes and chill for at least 4 hours before serving. This is a very rich pudding. You may like to serve coffee at the same time, to balance the richness.

JERUSALEM ARTICHOKE SOUP

1 lb Jerusalem artichokes
1 tsp vinegar
1 oz butter
1½ pints chicken stock
½ pint milk
salt, pepper

Scrub, peel and halve the artichokes. Soak them in cold water, with the vinegar, for 10 minutes. Drain well. Melt the butter in a thick pan. Add the artichokes and toss for a few minutes, then add the boiling stock. Season with salt and pepper. Bring back to the boil, and simmer, partially covered, for 40 minutes. Liquidize, or rub the mixture through a sieve. Blend in the warm milk and check the seasoning.

ESCALOPES WITH BLACK OLIVES

4 veal escalopes
2 oz butter
4 tbs oil
2 tbs flour
salt, pepper
4 tbs white wine, sherry
  or vermouth
1 tbs lemon juice
1 clove garlic
1 lemon
1 bay leaf
2 cloves
4 oz black olives

Flatten the escalopes lightly. Heat the butter and oil together in a thick frying pan. Put the flour, salt and pepper in a paper or plastic bag. Coat the escalopes with this seasoned flour by tossing them, one at a time, in the bag. Fry them in the butter and oil until golden brown, turning them once. Add the wine, lemon juice, crushed garlic, bay leaf and cloves. Cover the pan and allow to cook gently for 40–45 minutes. Add the stoned olives and cook for a further 2–3 minutes. Arrange the escalopes on a warm serving dish. Surround them with the olives and slices of lemon. Pour the sauce over before serving.

GREEN SALAD

1 cos lettuce
1 bunch watercress
2 heads chicory
1 clove garlic
½ cucumber
salt, pepper
6 tbs olive oil
2 tbs vinegar
½ tsp French mustard

Wash the lettuce and tear its leaves into pieces. Wash the watercress and tear it into manageable sprigs. Slice the chicory and peeled cucumber. Rub the salad bowl with a crushed clove of garlic. Place all the salad ingredients in it. Whisk together the oil, vinegar, salt, pepper and mustard. Pour this over the salad just before serving, and toss well.

CHOCOLATE AND ORANGE MOUSSE

4 oz rich plain chocolate
4 eggs
1 oz butter
1 orange or mandarin

Melt the chocolate in a low oven, or in a bowl in a pan of boiling water. Beat the egg yolks, and gradually add this mixture to the chocolate. Soften the butter and add it, bit by bit, to the chocolate mixture until well blended in. Stir in the juice of the orange or mandarin. Gently fold in the stiffly beaten egg whites until all traces of white have disappeared. Pour into cocotte dishes and chill for at least 2 hours before serving. Crystallized violets or rose petals make pretty garnishes for these individual mousses.

SPANISH OMELETTE

5 eggs
2 tomatoes
2 oz mushrooms
4 black olives
1 oz butter
2 oz bacon
1 large onion
1 clove garlic
½ green pepper
salt, pepper

Peel and slice the onion finely. Heat the butter in a large frying pan, and fry the sliced onion gently until golden. Add the peeled, sliced tomatoes, chopped bacon, sliced mushrooms, chopped pepper and crushed garlic. Season well with salt and pepper and allow to cook gently for 5 minutes. Add the halved, stoned olives. Beat the eggs lightly and pour them over the vegetables. Allow to cook gently until the bottom is quite set, lifting the sides from time to time to allow the unset mixture to run underneath. When the bottom is set, place the omelette under a hot grill for a few moments, to set the top. Serve hot or cold, topping each portion with a sprig of watercress or parsley.

MEAT LOAF WITH CREAM SAUCE

1 lb lean minced beef
1 lb lean minced pork
4 oz white breadcrumbs
salt, pepper
1 gill double cream
2 oz butter
2 eggs
herbs, fresh or dried
2 tbs milk

Soak the breadcrumbs in the milk. Blend them into the minced beef and pork. Season with salt, pepper and finely chopped herbs—parsley, thyme, marjoram or sage. Bind it with the beaten eggs. Blend the mixture well and form it into a loaf shape. Melt the butter in a roasting tray. Place the meat loaf in this and bake in a moderate oven for 1¼ hours. Stir the cream into the juices around the meat loaf, and return it to the oven for a further 15 minutes.

FRENCH BEAN SALAD

1½ lb French beans
2 tbs finely chopped
   parsley
2 cloves garlic
5 tbs olive oil
2 tbs vinegar
salt, pepper

Cook the beans in boiling salted water until tender but not too soft. Drain them and, while still hot, put them in a salad bowl. Mix together the oil, vinegar, crushed garlic and parsley. Toss the hot, drained beans in this dressing and chill before serving.

PINEAPPLE BASKETS

1 large, 2 medium or
   4 tiny pineapples

This is not so much a recipe as a method of serving fresh pineapple, so that it is pretty and easy to eat. Halve the pineapple lengthwise—if it is very large, quarter it lengthwise including the leaves. Using a very sharp grapefruit knife, penetrate the flesh of the pineapple just underneath the hard centre core. Cut all the way along, then down and along the bottom edge, just inside the prickly skin. Turn the half pineapple round and do the same at the other side. When this is complete it should be possible to remove all the tender flesh in one piece. But don't. Instead, cut it into neat, bite-size pieces, but leave it looking like an intact demi-pineapple. When the pineapple has been eaten you are left with a basket shape composed of the inedible parts of the fruit—the prickly skin, leaves and centre core. The prepared fruit might be sprinkled with brandy or liqueur, if liked. Kirsch blends particularly well with pineapple.

LENTIL SOUP

1 large onion
1 oz butter
1½ pints chicken stock
2 cupfuls lentils
salt, pepper

Heat the butter in a thick pan, and add the peeled and finely sliced onion. Toss over a gentle heat until golden. Remove from the heat and stir in the lentils, boiling stock, salt and pepper. Bring to the boil, half cover and allow to simmer gently, stirring often, until the lentils have become a smooth mass. This will probably take about 1 hour. Just before serving. stir in a large knob of butter. Scraps of bacon or ham could be added to the lentils during cooking to give a smoky flavour, but they should be discarded before serving.

NOISETTES D'AGNEAU EN BROCHETTE

8 lamb cutlets
6 rashers lean bacon
salt, pepper
1 lemon
marjoram

Dice the meat from the cutlets, so that, finally, you have 16–18 cubes of tender, fatless lamb. Cut the bacon rashers into pieces and thread alternate pieces of lamb and bacon onto small skewers. Season with salt, pepper, lemon juice and fresh marjoram, and grill for 8–10 minutes, under a hot grill, turning them from time to time.

GLOBE ARTICHOKES WITH VINAIGRETTE

4 globe artichokes
salt, pepper
½ lemon
6 tbs olive oil
2 tbs vinegar
½ tsp French mustard
1 clove garlic

Trim the stalks of the artichokes. Bring to the boil a large panful of salted water. Add the artichokes and ½ lemon. Bring back to the boil and allow to simmer until the artichokes are cooked. This will vary, of course, according to the size and condition of the artichoke, but should take between 25–35 minutes. The artichoke is cooked when a leaf can be detached cleanly and easily. Drain the artichokes, head downmost, in a colander, and allow to cool. Whisk together the oil, vinegar, mustard, salt, pepper and crushed garlic. Serve this dressing with the cooked, cold artichokes.

STRAWBERRIES WITH ORANGE

1 lb strawberries
2 oz castor sugar
1 orange

Sieve a third of the strawberries, pressing them through a nylon sieve with a wooden or plastic spoon. Do not use metal. Blend the sugar and juice of 1 orange into this purée, and place it in a serving dish. Top it with the whole, hulled strawberries. Serve cream separately.

OEUFS EN COCOTTE

4 eggs
4 tbs double cream
salt, pepper

Take 4 fireproof cocotte dishes. Place a tablespoonful of cream in each. Season them lightly with salt and pepper. Place the dishes in a shallow tray of hot water and put them in a moderate oven for a few minutes, until the cream is warm. Carefully break an egg into each dish, and top with an extra dab of cream. Bake in a moderate oven until the eggs have set lightly. This will vary, of course, according to the size of the egg, but should take 4–5 minutes. Serve immediately, with brown or granary bread and lots of unsalted butter.

BEEF AND POTATO GOULASH

1½ lb lean stewing beef
½ lb onions
½ lb potatoes
½ lb tomatoes
½ tsp salt
½ tbs paprika
2 tbs oil

Cut the meat into cubes. Heat the oil in a thick frying pan. Toss the beef and sliced onions in this until golden. Add the salt, peeled, quartered tomatoes and paprika. Add ½ gill water, stir well and transfer the mixture to an ovenware dish. Cover and cook in a moderate oven for 1½ hours. Peel the potatoes and cut them into small, irregular pieces. Stir them into the beef and onions and cook for a further 1 hour, stirring from time to time. By the time cooking is complete the liquid should have disappeared.

AVOCADO AND CUCUMBER SALAD

2 small ripe avocados
½ large cucumber
1 clove garlic
salt, pepper
6 dess olive oil
2 dess vinegar
pinch mustard powder

Peel the cucumber. Slice it very thinly. Place it in a colander, sprinkle it with salt, cover it with a weight and allow it to drain for 30 minutes. Whisk together the oil, vinegar, crushed garlic, salt, pepper and dried mustard. Peel the avocados. Slice them, not too thinly, and discard the stones. Gently blend together the cucumber, avocado and dressing.

RUMMY APPLES

1 lb Bramley apples
3 oz sugar
4 tsp rum

Peel, core and slice the apples. Place them in a saucepan together with the sugar. Cover with a tight-fitting lid, and cook over a very low flame until soft but not mushy—about 15 minutes. Stir a teaspoonful of rum into each serving. Serve either hot or cold, with cream.

ONION SOUP

1 large onion
1 oz butter
½ oz flour
1 pint beef stock
½ tsp Worcester sauce
salt, pepper

This is a recipe for a slow, oven-cooked soup which could be allowed to cook overnight, or put in the oven early in the morning and left unattended until needed in the evening. You will have to plan your other courses accordingly, though, if you cook the soup during the day, as you will not then be able to use the oven at a higher temperature for anything else. Slice the peeled onion finely. Heat the butter in a thick pan. Add the onion and toss over a low flame until golden. Remove from the heat and stir in the flour. Gradually add the stock, stirring all the time, then add the Worcester sauce, salt and pepper. Bring to the boil, transfer to an ovenware casserole, cover with a well-fitting lid and cook in a very cool oven—Gas Mark ¼ or 150–165 deg. F.—for 8–10 hours. This soup will not suffer in the least if left for an hour or two longer.

HAM LOAF

2 lb lean pork
1 lb lean boiled ham
1 cupful brown bread-
    crumbs
2 eggs
milk
salt, pepper

Mince the ham and pork together. Blend in the fine brown breadcrumbs. Bind with the well-beaten eggs. Season to taste and stir in a small cupful of milk. Press the mixture into a buttered loaf tin. Bake in a moderate oven for 1½ hours. Pour off any fat and return to the oven for a final 5 minutes.

ARTICHOKES IN TOMATO JUICE

2 lb Jerusalem artichokes
1 oz butter
1 tbs oil
½ pint tomato juice
salt, pepper
1 small onion
dill, fresh or dried

Select artichokes of a similar size and shape, if possible. Peel and halve, or quarter them, depending on their size. Heat the butter and oil in a thick pan. Add the artichokes and toss well for a few minutes. Then add the peeled, sliced onion and allow to cook for a further 3–4 minutes. Pour in the tomato juice, season with salt and pepper and bring to the boil. Allow to simmer gently until the artichokes are cooked, testing with a skewer and removing those which are cooked before they disintegrate. When all the artichokes are cooked arrange them in a serving dish. Boil up the sauce for 4–5 minutes, then pour this over the artichokes and top with a sprinkling of chopped dill.

CHRISTMAS ICE CREAM

1 pint vanilla ice cream
½ lb mincemeat
2 tbs brandy

Heat the mincemeat and brandy together in a thick pan. Just before serving, pour it over portions of vanilla ice cream, either bought or home-made.

EGGS WITH SKORDALIA

4 eggs
1 egg yolk
2 cloves garlic
salt, pepper
1 gill oil
2 oz breadcrumbs
2 oz ground almonds
lemon juice
parsley

Hardboil the eggs and shell them under cold, running water. Pound the garlic to a fine pulp. Stir in the egg yolk. Season well with salt and pepper, and stir well. Gradually add the oil, drop by drop, until the mixture begins to thicken, then add the oil more rapidly. Blend in the breadcrumbs and ground almonds. Add lemon juice and finely chopped parsley to taste, and serve this sauce with the hardboiled eggs.

RED MULLET 'FOILED'

4 red mullet
2 small onions
1 lemon
2 oz butter
4 sprigs rosemary

Take 4 squares of aluminium foil, each large enough to envelop a fish. Butter them well. Place a cleaned mullet on each. Top each with ½ sliced onion, a sprig of rosemary, 2–3 slivers of lemon peel and ½ oz butter. Close the foil carefully, making sure that there are no gaps for precious juices to escape. Bake on a baking sheet in a low oven for 30 minutes.

FRENCH BEANS WITH CREAM

1 lb French beans
3 oz butter
½ gill double cream
salt

Slice the beans finely and boil them in salted water for 15 minutes, then drain them well. Place them in a pan together with 2 oz butter. Cover with a tight-fitting lid and allow to cook gently for 10 minutes. Heat the cream, pour it over the beans and allow to cook for 2–3 minutes, then stir in the remaining butter and a good sprinkling of salt before serving.

KAY FRUIT SALAD

2 oz icing sugar
1 gill cold water
2 oranges
2 apples
2 pears
2 bananas
grapes

The basic recipe started off as my grandmother's, with each generation embroidering it a little more. Put the sugar and water in a serving bowl, and stir until the sugar has dissolved. Peel the bananas, and cut them into thin slices, add them to the syrup. Peel the apples, and grate them coarsely into the syrup. Add the pears, peeled and cut into tiny pieces. Add the grapes, halved, skinned and seeded. Halve the oranges. Scoop out all the flesh with a grapefruit knife, then separate each segment and add it to the rest of the fruit. Squeeze the juice from the empty skins into the mixture. Stir well and chill before serving. Obviously the recipe lends itself to all sorts of variation, according to the fruit available. The secret, though, is to be painstaking in its preparation—no skin, no pith, no pips, and all the fruit cut into very small, neat pieces.

CHIFFONADE

1 lettuce heart
1 oz rice
1 pint chicken stock
1 oz butter
salt, pepper

Wash, shake and shred the lettuce. Heat the butter in a thick pan. Add the shredded lettuce and cook gently for 10 minutes, stirring from time to time. Add the rice and boiling stock. Season with salt and pepper, and cook until the rice is tender. **Serve piping hot.**

STEAK AND PIMENTO PIE

½ lb left over stewed steak,
   or steak and kidney
1 small tin red peppers
salt, pepper
parsley
lemon thyme
6 oz short pastry

Mince together the steak, gravy and the tinned peppers. Add some finely chopped parsley, a little lemon thyme, salt and pepper. Arrange the mixture in a pie dish, cover it with a short pastry lid **and bake in a moderate oven for 30–35 minutes.**

MIXED CUCUMBER SALAD

½ fresh cucumber
3 large pickled cucumbers
1 small onion
salt, pepper
6 dess olive oil
2 dess vinegar

Peel and finely chop the fresh cucumber. Chop the pickled cucumbers, without peeling them. Blend them together. Stir in the very finely chopped onion. Mix together the oil, vinegar, salt and pepper. Pour this over the cucumber and stir well.

CHARLOTTE RUSSE

1 egg white
½ pint double cream
2 tbs castor sugar
1 tbs brandy or liqueur
   of choice
sponge fingers

Whip the cream. Beat the egg white until stiff, and fold it into the cream. Fold in the sugar and liqueur or brandy. Line a mould, or individual glasses with sponge fingers, trimming them to size if necessary. Fill with the cream and chill well before serving.

CURRIED AUBERGINES

2 medium aubergines
1 small onion
oil
curry powder
½ glassful sherry
parsley
2 lemons
salt, pepper
parsley

Peel and thickly slice the aubergines. Sprinkle them with salt and allow to stand in a colander for 1 hour. Heat 2 tbs oil in a thick pan. Add the aubergine slices and fry gently until lightly browned. Remove them from the pan. Fry the peeled and sliced onion in the oil until golden. Sprinkle in 1 dessertspoonful of curry powder. Stir well, then blend in the sherry and the juice of 1 lemon. Season with salt and pepper. Return the aubergines to the pan, and allow to simmer for 5 minutes. Transfer the mixture to a serving dish and allow to cool. Sprinkle with finely chopped parsley, and serve with lemon quarters.

VEAL WITH PINEAPPLE

4 veal escalopes
4 oz mushrooms
4 pineapple rings
1 gill cream
1½ oz butter

Cut the veal into thin strips. Heat the butter in a thick frying pan. Add the veal strips and the sliced mushrooms, and toss them over a gentle heat until cooked. Transfer them to a serving dish and keep them warm. Add the pineapple rings to the pan and heat them thoroughly, then arrange them on top of the veal and mushrooms. Add the cream to the juices in the pan and heat gently, stirring all the time. Pour this sauce over the meat and pineapple before serving.

FOILED ONIONS

8 medium onions
salt, pepper
2 oz butter
fresh tarragon or basil

Butter 8 pieces of foil, each large enough to envelop an onion. Place an unpeeled onion on each. Season with salt and pepper and a few tarragon or basil leaves. Fold over the foil so that no precious juices can escape. Arrange the foiled onions on a baking tray and bake in a moderate oven for 1–1¼ hours.

VANILLA MOUSSE

½ pint double cream
1 egg white
½ tsp vanilla essence
salt
1 oz icing sugar

Whip the cream until stiff. Fold in the sifted icing sugar, vanilla essence and a pinch of salt. Fold in the stiffly beaten egg white. Chill for at least 2 hours before serving with ratafias or sponge fingers and perhaps some fresh strawberries or raspberries.

QUICHE LORRAINE

½ lb short pastry
5 rashers lean bacon
½ pint double cream
1 egg
3 egg yolks
salt, pepper

Line a flan ring with the short pastry, and chill it in the refrigerator while preparing the filling. Dice the bacon, discarding the rind, and fry it lightly. Arrange it in the bottom of the flan ring. Whisk together the cream, egg and egg yolks. Season with salt and pepper, bearing in mind the saltness of the bacon. Pour this into the flan and bake in a hot oven for 20 minutes, then reduce the heat for a further 10–15 minutes. Serve warm.

GIGOT D'AGNEAU A LA PROVENCALE

1 small leg of lamb, boned and rolled
3 aubergines
1 lb tomatoes
4 oz green olives
1 gill oil
2 cloves garlic
salt, pepper

With the point of a sharp knife, make some small slits in the leg of lamb. Into each insert a small sliver of peeled garlic. Roast the lamb in your usual way. Meanwhile, slice the aubergines, sprinkle them with coarse salt and allow them to drain for 1 hour. Peel the tomatoes, quarter them and fry them in a little oil for 4–5 minutes, together with 1 crushed clove of garlic, salt and pepper. Heat 4 tbs oil in a thick pan, add the aubergines and fry them until golden and tender. Blend in the stoned olives and the fried tomatoes, and keep this mixture hot while carving the meat. Arrange the carved meat on a serving dish, surround it with the aubergine mixture and sprinkle with plenty of finely chopped parsley.

CUCUMBER AND CREAM SALAD

2 cucumbers
1 lemon
dill, fresh or dried
salt, pepper
3 tbs double cream

Peel the cucumbers. Cut them into thick slices. Pour boiling water over them, allow to stand for 1 minute, then refresh in plenty of cold water. Drain well. Allow to cool, then blend in the cream, the juice of 1 lemon, salt and pepper. Blend well. Serve sprinkled with plenty of fresh or dried dill.

GREEK FRUIT SALAD

2 bananas
1 apple
2 oranges
2 tbs brandy
8 fl oz natural yogurt
4 oz castor sugar

Peel the fruit and cut it into small pieces. Stir in the brandy. Mix well and allow to stand in a cool place for at least 1 hour. Beat together the sugar and yogurt. Stir this lightly into the fruit. Serve chilled.

POTATO SOUP WITH CELERIAC

2 lb potatoes
½ oz butter
1 small celeriac
1 pint stock, chicken
   or beef
salt, pepper

Peel and slice the potatoes and celeriac. Allow them to simmer in the stock until tender. Add the butter and season well with salt and pepper. Liquidize, or rub the mixture through a sieve. Check the seasoning, and thin the soup down with a little cream or top of the milk if it appears too thick.

BOEUF STROGANOFF

1 lb beef fillet
4 oz button mushrooms
2 onions
3 oz butter
¾ gill double cream
tomato purée
salt, pepper
cayenne pepper

Cut the meat into strips like fat matchsticks. Melt half the butter in a pan. Fry the finely chopped onions in this until lightly browned, then add the thinly sliced mushrooms. Cover the pan and allow to cook for 2 minutes. Heat the remaining butter in a second pan. When hot, add the strips of beef and fry them very quickly until brown but not dry. Add the mushrooms and onions. Blend in 2 soupspoonfuls of tomato purée, a pinch of cayenne pepper, salt and pepper. Stir well, cover the pan and allow to simmer gently for 25 minutes. Stir in the warmed cream before serving.

CAULIFLOWER WITH ONIONS

1 large cauliflower
2 large onions
salt, pepper
1½ oz butter

Separate the cauliflower into sprigs. Allow them to soak in lukewarm salted water for 15 minutes. Drain well, then plunge them into boiling salted water and allow to cook gently for 10–15 minutes. Do not allow the cauliflower to become too soft. Meanwhile, peel and slice the onion into rings. Fry them in butter until soft and golden. Drain the cooked cauliflower, and top it with the onion rings.

PINEAPPLE AND ORANGE SALAD

1 medium pineapple
3 large oranges
2 oz crystallized ginger

Cut up the pineapple into bite-size pieces, discarding any tough bits. Halve the oranges. Scoop out the flesh with a grapefruit knife, then remove all the segments carefully, without any pips or membrane. Add them to the pineapple, together with the finely chopped ginger. Mix well and chill before serving.

POTAGE VERONIQUE

2 oz butter
2 medium onions
1 lb tomatoes
1 tbs tomato purée
1 bay leaf
1 clove garlic
6 peppercorns
salt
1½ pints chicken stock
1 tbs rice
parsley
1 tsp sugar

Heat the butter in a thick pan. Add the peeled, sliced onions and ¾ lb of the tomatoes, not skinned, but chopped roughly. Stir in the tomato purée, bay leaf, crushed garlic, peppercorns and a large pinch of salt. Cover the pan and allow to cook slowly for 10 minutes, stirring occasionally. Rub the mixture through a sieve. Place the sieved mixture in a clean pan, add the stock and stir over the heat until the mixture comes to the boil. Add the rice, previously boiled in salted water for 10 minutes. Simmer for 15 minutes. Skin and finely chop the remaining tomatoes. Add them to the soup together with some finely chopped parsley and the sugar. Check the seasoning before serving.

VEAL WITH CREAM AND CUCUMBER

4 veal escalopes
4 oz butter
1 gill cream
1 medium cucumber
paprika
salt, pepper

Peel the cucumber, and cut it into 1-inch lengths. Boil them in salted water for 10–15 minutes, until tender, then drain them and keep them warm. Heat 2 oz butter in a thick frying pan. When hot add the seasoned escalopes and cook until brown on both sides, then reduce and cook more gently until the meat is quite tender and thoroughly cooked. Remove the escalopes and keep them warm. Scrape the pan well to get all the juices together, then add the cream, 1 dessertspoonful of paprika, salt and pepper. Bring to the boil, cook quickly for a few minutes, then blend in 2 oz butter and the cooked cucumber. Reheat gently, and pour all this sauce and cucumber over the veal before serving.

CAROTTES A LA VICHY

1 lb carrots
2 oz butter
½ tsp sugar
salt
chopped parsley

Peel and thinly slice the carrots. Place them in a wide saucepan, together with the butter, sugar and salt. Add sufficient water to barely cover the carrots. Cook over a very high flame to evaporate the water, then reduce the heat and allow to cook gently until tender. Sprinkle with finely chopped parsley just before serving.

BROWN BREAD ICE CREAM

3 oz wholemeal or
   granary bread
½ pint double cream
1 oz castor sugar
1 tbs orange or lemon
   juice
3 tbs clear honey

Slice the bread and discard the crusts. Dry the bread in a very low oven for 20–25 minutes, then crumble it. The 'crumbling' can be done in a liquidizer or by wrapping the bread in a cloth and hitting it with a rolling pin. Whisk together the cream and castor sugar, and place it in the freezing compartment of the refrigerator for 30 minutes. Warm the honey in a pan. Add the orange juice, and pour this mixture over the breadcrumbs. Blend in the chilled cream and mix well. Pour the mixture into the ice-making tray. Cover it with foil and freeze for 3 hours, agitating it with a fork twice during the freezing period.

PRAWNS WITH BAKED EGGS

3 oz peeled prawns
4 eggs
4 tbs double cream
pepper
1 oz butter

Take 4 cocotte dishes. Put a small knob of butter and some prawns in each. Place the cocotte dishes in a baking tray. Pour a little water into the baking tray. Heat in a moderate oven for 5 minutes. Remove from the oven and carefully break an egg into each dish. Cover with a table-spoonful of cream and sprinkle with freshly milled pepper. Return to the oven—still in the baking tray—for a further 7–8 minutes, or until the eggs are set, but not hard.

TURKISH PILAFF

4 tbs oil
½ lb Italian or short grain rice
salt, pepper
1 clove garlic
1 tbs currants
1 tbs raisins
2 onions
pine kernels or almonds
2 cupfuls cooked lamb and/or garlic sausage
2 tomatoes
sour cream or natural yogurt

Heat 2 tbs oil in a thick pan. Add the rice, and stir it over the heat until the rice becomes transparent. Pour in 4 pints boiling salted water and cook quickly for 12 minutes. Meanwhile, dice the meat and/or garlic sausage. Heat the remaining oil in a second pan. Add the peeled and sliced onion and crushed garlic. Cook until tender, then add the skinned and chopped tomatoes, raisins, currants, lamb, sausage, a few pine kernels or almonds, salt and pepper. Toss until well mixed and hot. Blend this into the cooked and drained rice. Serve with a bowl of sour cream or natural yogurt.

PEPPER AND OLIVE SALAD

2 red peppers
2 green peppers
salt, pepper
sugar
4 tbs olive oil
2 tbs vinegar
1 oz green olives
1 oz black olives

Cut the peppers into rings, discarding the seeds. Pour boiling water over them for 2 minutes, then rinse in cold water. Blend in the stoned olives. Mix together the oil, vinegar, salt, pepper and a pinch of castor sugar. Pour this over the peppers and olives and serve at once.

CAMILLE FRUITS

1½ lb mixed fresh straw-berries
melon, pears, raspberries peaches, tangerines, etc.
¾ pint double cream
1½ tbs clear honey
½ gill brandy or rum
toasted almond nibs

Prepare the chosen fruit, and cut it into pieces as though for fruit salad. Whisk together the honey and cream. Fold in the brandy. Stir the fruit into this cream, arrange it in a serving dish and garnish it with toasted almond nibs.

SHRIMP AND CUCUMBER SOUP

1 pint yogurt
1 gill double cream
1 large cucumber
½ pint shrimps
salt, pepper
1 clove garlic
mint

Mix together the yogurt and cream. Peel the cucumber and shred it into fine slivers. Stir it into the yogurt. Add the shrimps, salt, pepper and a tablespoonful of finely chopped fresh mint. Chill this until needed.
Just before serving, rub the serving tureen or individual soup bowls with a cut clove of garlic. Pour in the soup, and garnish with a little more chopped, fresh mint.

PORK WITH CORIANDER

1½ lb pork fillet
1 tbs ground coriander
    seeds
red wine
salt, pepper

Cut the meat into smallish pieces, discarding any fat or gristle. Put the meat in a basin, and mix it well with the ground coriander seeds. Barely cover with red wine and allow to stand for 24 hours. Transfer the meat and wine to an ovenware dish and cover it with a tight-fitting lid. Cook in a low oven for 2–2½ hours.

JACKET POTATOES

4 large potatoes
salt, pepper
3 oz butter
paprika
parsley
chives
lemon thyme

Select potatoes of a similar size and shape if possible. Scrub them well, and dry. Rub the skins with a greased paper. Bake them in a moderate oven, just resting on an oven shelf, for 45–60 minutes. The potatoes are cooked when soft to the touch. Soften the butter. Blend in a large pinch of paprika, and 2 tbs of finely chopped mixed chives, parsley and thyme. Prick the top of each potato in the form of a cross. Squeeze the sides of the potatoes gently . The cross should open at each point. Place a large knob of the herb butter atop each potato before serving.

CREAM CHEESE CAKE

1 lb cream cheese
6 oz castor sugar
2 eggs
1 gill double cream
1 lemon
½ pint milk
2 dess gelatine
salt

for topping:
4 oz digestive biscuits
1½ oz butter
1 oz castor sugar

In a saucepan place 5 oz sugar, gelatine and a pinch of salt. Beat together the egg yolks and milk, and gradually add them to the gelatine. Bring gently to the boil, stirring all the time, but do not allow the mixture to bubble. Remove from the heat and blend in the grated rind of 1 lemon and 2 tbs fresh lemon juice. Allow it to cool until it begins to set, then blend in the cream cheese. Whisk the egg whites until stiff. Fold in the remaining 1 oz sugar and whisk again. Fold this into the cheese mixture. Also fold in the whipped cream. Rinse out a ring mould in cold water. Pour in the cheese mixture. Crush the digestive biscuits, either in a liquidizer or, wrapped in a cloth and crushed with a rolling pin. Blend the melted butter and sugar into the biscuit crumbs, and top the cheese mixture with them. Chill for at least 2 hours. Turn out on to a plate, wrapping a hot cloth round the mould to facilitate the unmoulding.

OEUFS A LA NEIGE

4 eggs
salt, pepper
sprigs thyme
1 oz butter

Separate the eggs, placing an egg yolk in each of 4 fireproof cocotte dishes. Whisk the combined egg whites until stiff, and pile a large spoonful on top of each egg yolk. Season each with salt, pepper and a tiny sprig of thyme. Dot each with a small nut of butter. Place the dishes in a tray of hot water, and bake in a moderate oven until set and golden.

DAUBE A LA CORSOISE

2 lb rolled rib of beef
½ lb mushrooms
¼ lb bacon, in the piece
4 large tomatoes
4 oz black olives
1 lb new potatoes
1 small glassful whisky
2 tbs olive oil
sprig thyme
salt, pepper

Season the beef with salt and pepper. Heat the oil in a deep, narrow pan. Toss the beef in this until brown all over. Add the bacon, cut into small pieces, the peeled and quartered tomatoes, 2–3 cloves of garlic, salt, pepper, thyme and the stoned olives. Pour over the whisky. Cover the pan and cook in a low oven for 2 hours, then add the potatoes, previously peeled, sliced and cooked in oil or butter until almost tender. Also add the halved mushrooms and cook for a further 15 minutes.

POLISH CAULIFLOWER

1 large cauliflower
salt, pepper
2 oz butter
2 oz fresh breadcrumbs
1 egg

Hardboil the egg. Shell and chop it finely. Divide the cauliflower into florets, and cook them in boiling salted water for 10–15 minutes. Drain them well and transfer them to a serving dish. Fry the breadcrumbs in the butter until brown and crisp. Blend in the finely chopped egg and a sprinkling of black pepper. Top the cooked cauliflower with this mixture before serving.

ATHOLL BROSE

½ pint double cream
4 oz fine oatmeal
4 oz clear honey
1 gill whisky

Whisk the cream to a froth. Toast the oatmeal lightly under the grill, taking great care that it does not burn. Fold the oatmeal, honey and whisky into the cream. Blend well and chill before serving.

SMOKED TROUT QUICHE

1 smoked trout
2 eggs
8 fl oz double cream
pepper
parsley
8 oz short pastry

Roll out the pastry, line a flan ring with it and place in the refrigerator while preparing the filling. Whisk together the eggs and cream. Season with plenty of freshly milled black pepper and 1 tbs finely chopped parsley. Flake the flesh of the smoked trout, discarding skin and bones. This is best done with well-scrubbed hands, which can 'feel out' the bones more easily. Blend the flaked fish into the egg mixture, pour into the flan cases and bake in a moderate oven for 30–35 minutes.
Serve hot or warm, but preferably not cold.

CHICKEN PILAFF

1 roasting chicken
1 pint chicken stock
4 oz butter
salt, pepper
3 oz flaked almonds
3 oz seeded raisins
3 tbs coconut
½ tsp curry powder
¾ lb Italian rice

Joint the chicken. Heat the chicken stock, add the pieces of chicken and allow them to simmer gently, covered, until quite tender. Heat the butter in a large sauté pan, add the pieces of cooked chicken, and keep them warm in this while cooking the rice in the boiling chicken stock. The rice should be tender but not mushy. Remove the chicken from the sauté pan, and keep it warm. Fry half of the boiled rice in the butter, together with the almonds, raisins, coconut and curry powder. Stir well over the heat, then pop this mixture into a hot oven, or under the grill, until it becomes brown and crispy on top. In a deep serving dish arrange the plain boiled rice, cover it with the pieces of chicken, then top it with the fried rice and raisin mixture.

CHICORY AND WATERCRESS SALAD

1 lb chicory
1 bunch watercress
salt, pepper
6 tbs olive oil
2 tbs vinegar
½ tsp mustard

Trim the chicory of outside leaves. Cut it into thin slices. Wash and drain the watercress, and cut it into small pieces. Add it to the chicory. Sprinkle with salt. Blend together the mustard, salt, pepper, oil and vinegar, and pour this over the chicory and watercress. Toss well before serving.

LAYERED APPLES

2 lb eating apples
1 gill sweet cider or water
4 tbs castor sugar

for crumb mixture:
3 tbs fresh breadcrumbs
4 oz butter
2 tbs sugar

Peel, core and slice the apples. Cook them gently with the sugar and cider until of a dry purée consistency. In a second pan place the butter, breadcrumbs and sugar. Mix well over a low flame for 5 minutes. Allow to cool. Fill a serving dish with alternate layers of apple purée and crumb mixture, finishing with a layer of crumbs. Decorate with whipped cream.

CHILLED AVOCADO SOUP

1 large avocado
1½ gills chicken stock
5 tbs double cream
3 tbs single cream
cucumber
lemon juice
salt, pepper
1 shallot
paprika

Peel and slice the very ripe avocado. Discard the stone. In a liquidizer or blender place the sliced avocado, stock, cream, salt, pepper, a piece of unpeeled cucumber ¾-inch long, a chopped shallot or tiny onion and 1 teaspoonful of lemon juice. Liquidize. Check the seasoning before chilling well. Sprinkle with a pinch of paprika before serving.

PAUPIETTES OF BEEF

4 thin slices of lean beef
4 oz bacon
1 small onion
2 oz mushrooms
2 tbs chopped parsley
1 oz butter
1 tsp French mustard
1 tbs tomato purée
½ lemon
Worcester sauce
½ pint good gravy

Mince the bacon. Add the chopped onion, chopped mushrooms, parsley, French mustard and ½ oz butter. Season with salt, pepper and a dash of Worcester sauce. Toss this mixture in a frying pan for a few moments. Trim the beef slices. Spread the bacon mixture on each slice, roll them up, tie them with string or cotton, and fry them in the remaining butter over a high flame until brown all over. Add the tomato purée and the juice of ½ lemon to the gravy, and bring this liquid to the boil. Pour it over the paupiettes and cook, covered, in a moderate oven for 1½ hours. Remove the string or cotton from each paupiette before serving.

AUBERGINE PUREE

2 large aubergines
1 onion
½ gill olive oil
½ lemon
salt, pepper
1 clove garlic
1 tbs finely chopped
  parsley

Remove the aubergine stalks. Grill the aubergines until the skins crack and turn brown. Skin them. Pound the flesh in a liquidizer. Add the finely grated onion and the crushed garlic. Continue to pound or liquidize the mixture until it is smooth. Season with salt and pepper. Gradually add the oil, drop by drop, stirring all the time. When the mixture begins to thicken add the oil in a thin trickle, still stirring. Stir in the juice of ½ lemon and the parsley. Serve very cold.

BAKED APRICOTS

1 lb apricots
3 oz vanilla sugar*

Arrange the apricots in an ovenproof dish. Sprinkle them with 1 tbs water and the vanilla sugar. Bake in a very low oven for 1 hour. Serve with pouring cream.

*Vanilla sugar can be bought, at great expense, or made, by storing a vanilla pod in an airtight container of castor sugar. The vanilla pod flavours the sugar, and will not need replacing for months. Just fill up with more sugar as it is needed.

HUNGARIAN SALAD

4 oz sliced garlic
 sausage
4 oz lean boiled ham
1 pickled cucumber
4 inch fresh cucumber
3 tbs oil
1 tbs vinegar
salt, pepper

Cut the sausage, ham, pickled cucumber and fresh cucumber into smallish pieces. Whisk together the oil, vinegar, salt and pepper, and pour this over the meat and cucumber. Blend well.

CORNISH PASTIES

1 lb self raising flour
8 oz butter
salt
water

1 lb lean lamb or beef
2 medium potatoes
salt, pepper
1 large onion
chopped mixed herbs

Make the pastry in the usual manner, and roll it out to a thickness of ¼ inch, and cut it into rounds, 6 inches in diameter. (A saucepan lid would be useful for cutting out these pastry rounds.) On to each *half* circle put a layer of finely sliced raw potato, onion, herbs and finely diced or minced meat, all well seasoned. Damp the edges of the pastry. Fold over into a semi-circle and press the edges together well, crimping them. Make a small slit in the top of each, and bake in a moderate oven for 45–60 minutes.

COURGETTES AND TOMATOES

1 lb courgettes
2 large tomatoes
salt, pepper
1 oz butter

Slice the courgettes. Place them in a colander and sprinkle them with salt. Allow to stand for 30 minutes, then place them in a thick saucepan, together with the butter and peeled, chopped tomatoes. Allow to cook gently for 10–15 minutes, by which time the courgettes should be tender but not mushy.

BANANAS WITH RUM AND CREAM

6 large ripe bananas
3 tbs rum
½ pint double cream
2 oz icing sugar
chocolate

Peel and slice the bananas. Pour over them the cream, rum and sifted icing sugar. Toss them well, so that all the banana slices are well coated. Arrange them in a serving dish and sprinkle with grated chocolate.

CROUTE AU JAMBON

4 oz boiled ham
3 oz butter
4 tbs creamed horse-
  radish
4 tbs double cream
bread
garlic

Cut the ham into thin strips. Heat 1 oz butter in a thick pan and warm the ham strips in this. Blend in the creamed horseradish and cream. Rub a saucer with a cut clove of garlic. Cream the softened butter to a paste on this garlicky saucer. Toast some slices of bread. Cut them into fancy shapes, spread with the garlic butter, then with the hot horseradish ham, and serve immediately.

BRAZILIAN POUSSINS

4 poussins
1 large packet frozen
  petits pois
4 oz lean boiled ham
3 oz brazil nuts
1 cupful brown bread-
  crumbs
2 tbs cream

Cook the peas according to the instructions on the packet, then purée them. To this purée add the finely sliced nuts, the ham cut into tiny cubes, the breadcrumbs and the cream. Mix well, and use this stuffing to fill each poussin. Roast them, covered in foil, in a moderate oven for 45–50 minutes, removing the foil for the final few minutes of cooking.

STUFFED TOMATOES

6 large tomatoes
1 slice white bread
2 tbs ground almonds
1 clove garlic
salt, pepper
parsley
1 tbs oil

Slice the tops off the tomatoes. Scoop out the pulp. Blend together the breadcrumbs, ground almonds, salt, pepper, the crushed garlic clove and 1 tbs finely chopped parsley. Add the finely chopped tomato pulp and mix well. Fill the hollowed tomatoes with this mixture, sprinkle each with a few drops of oil and bake in a moderate oven for 20–25 minutes.

LEMON ICE CREAM

3 oz castor sugar
1 large lemon
3 egg yolks
¾ pint single cream

Grate the lemon rind and stir it into the cream. Whisk together the egg yolks and sugar and blend them into the lemon cream. Stir this mixture in a thick pan over a very low heat until it has the consistency of a thin custard. Do not allow it to boil. Remove the pan from the heat, strain the custard through a sieve and allow it to cool. Blend in the strained juice of ½ lemon. Pour this mixture into an ice-making tray, cover it with foil and freeze at maximum temperature for 2½ hours, agitating it twice during freezing.

84

CARROT AND ORANGE SOUP

1 lb carrots
2 onions
2 oranges
2 oz butter
1 pint stock
1 gill cream
salt, pepper
parsley

Peel and slice the carrots and onions. Heat the butter in a saucepan, and toss the carrots in this until tender, but not brown. Add the boiling stock (preferably chicken) salt, and pepper. Allow to simmer gently for 20–25 minutes. Either liquidize the soup, or press it through a sieve. Allow the resulting purée to cool completely before adding the juice of 2 oranges, a little chopped parsley and the cream. Stir well, and serve cold. If you store this soup in the refrigerator, remember to remove it about 30 minutes before serving.

PORK AND PRUNES

2 medium pork fillets
2 tsp cornflour
10–12 large prunes
1 gill sherry or vermouth
2 onions
6 oz mushrooms
½ pint chicken stock or
    water
fresh thyme
2 oz butter

Soak the prunes in the sherry for 4 hours. Remove any fat from the pork, then cut the fillets into four and slice them thinly lengthwise. Heat the butter in a thick pan. Fry the peeled and sliced onions in this until transparent. Add the pork. Fry lightly, then add the sliced mushrooms, salt, pepper and a pinch of fresh thyme. Pour in the prunes, sherry and stock or water. Bring to the boil, cover and allow to simmer gently for 40 minutes. Dissolve the cornflour in a little water, then blend this into the sauce. Bring back to the boil and cook for a further 5 minutes before serving.

CABBAGE AND CREAM

1 medium white cabbage
1 oz butter
¾ gill double cream
salt, pepper
1 tbs caraway seeds

Shred the cabbage finely. Plunge it into rapidly boiling salted water for 7 minutes. Drain it well. Heat the butter in a thick pan. Add the cabbage, toss it well, then stir in the cream. Bring it gently to simmering point then remove from the heat and stir in salt, pepper and the caraway seeds, before serving.

VIENNESE BISCUIT CAKE

4½ oz plain chocolate
½ lb digestive biscuits
2 oz butter
2 tbs golden syrup

Crush the biscuits to a fine powder, either in the liquidizer or wrapped in a tea towel and crushed with a rolling pin. Break up the chocolate and place it in a pan, together with the syrup and butter. Heat gently until the butter and chocolate have dissolved completely and the mixture is well blended. Stir in the powdered biscuits and stir over a low heat until the mixture forms a smooth paste. Press the mixture into a lightly oiled flan ring and allow to set for 1 hour, before turning out and serving with whipped cream.

MUSHROOMS EN CROUTE

1 lb button mushrooms
1 Vienna loaf
½ gill double cream
3 oz butter
salt, pepper

for garlic butter:
4 oz butter
2 cloves garlic
salt, pepper

Slice the top off the loaf, and scoop out its crumb, reserving it for use in stuffings, or for coating fish or veal. Blend the crushed garlic into the softened butter. Season with salt and pepper. Spread this garlic butter all over the inside of the scooped-out loaf. Place it in a hot oven for 10–15 minutes. Meanwhile, toss the mushrooms in 3 oz butter until cooked. Season them with salt and pepper, and blend in the warmed cream. Pour the mushrooms into the garlic loaf, and serve very hot, cut into slices.

DEVILLED CUTLETS

8 lamb cutlets
2 tsp Worcester sauce
2 tsp mushroom ketchup
salt, pepper
cayenne pepper
4 oz butter
1 tbs dry mustard

Trim the cutlets and grill them on both sides in the usual way. Mix together all the other ingredients and spread them over the cooked cutlets just before serving.

CABBAGE WITH CHEESE SAUCE

1 medium cabbage
2 stalks celery
½ pint basic white sauce
2 oz grated cheese
2 oz fresh breadcrumbs
1 oz flaked almonds
1 oz butter

Shred the cabbage and celery. Cook it in boiling, salted water for 10 minutes. Drain it well. To the hot, white sauce add the grated cheese, and stir well. Blend the drained cabbage and celery into this hot sauce and arrange it in an ovenware dish. Sprinkle with the breadcrumbs and flaked almonds. Dot with nuts of butter and bake in a hot oven until golden and crispy.

GREEK EGG CUSTARD

1 pint milk
3 oz castor sugar
1 tbs double cream
2 tbs brandy
6 egg yolks
3 egg whites

Take a 1½–2 pint straight-sided soufflé dish. In it place the sugar, cream, egg yolks and egg whites. Beat them vigorously for 2 minutes. Scald the milk and add it to the mixture, stirring all the time. Stir in the brandy. Stand the dish in a tray of water and bake in a fairly low oven for 20–25 minutes. Cool, then chill before serving. This custard has a very delicate flavour, and should not be served with anything pungent or powerful. A slice of Madeira cake, or a few sponge fingers would partner it ideally.

MIXED FRUIT JUICE

1 grapefruit
2 oranges
2 tangerines
1 lemon
sugar
cocktail cherries

Blend together the squeezed juice of the grapefruit, lemon, oranges and tangerines. Sweeten to taste and stir well to dissolve the sugar. Chill. Serve in chilled glasses, each garnished with a cherry on a cocktail stick.

KIDNEY, PORK AND BEAN HOTPOT

½ lb ox kidney
½ lb lean pork
½ lb haricot beans
2 onions
2 carrots
1 oz butter
1 tbs oil
salt, pepper
6 juniper berries
½ pint dry cider
½ pint tomato juice
2 tsp French mustard

Soak the beans in cold water overnight. Drain them, put them in a pan, cover with fresh cold water, bring to the boil and allow to simmer, *unsalted*, for 1 hour. Dice the kidney, discarding any fat or gristle. Soak the kidney in lightly salted water for 30 minutes. Heat the butter and oil in a frying pan, and fry the chopped onions and carrots in this. Transfer these vegetables to a dish and keep them warm, while frying the diced pork, and dried kidney in the same pan. Season with salt, pepper and crushed juniper berries. Fill an ovenware dish with alternate layers of drained beans, meat and vegetables. End with a layer of beans. Pour the cider into the pan in which the frying was done. Stir well to incorporate all the juices, blend in the tomato juice, bring to the boil and pour this over the beans. Cover with a close fitting lid, and cook in a very low oven, Reg. 1 for 3 hours. Stir in the mustard just before serving.

TOMATO SALAD WITH CREAM

¾ lb large tomatoes
1½ gills double cream
salt, pepper
fresh tarragon or chives

Peel the tomatoes. Slice them into a shallow serving dish. Chop a few tarragon leaves very finely, and blend them into the cream, together with a good sprinkling of coarse salt and freshly ground black pepper. Pour this cream over the tomatoes immediately before serving.

CREAMY APPLE FLAN

½ lb short pastry
1 lb cooking apples
3 oz sugar
½ oz flour
salt
cinnamon
1 gill double cream

Line a flan ring with the short pastry and bake it blind, for 10–15 minutes. Peel, core and thickly slice the apples. Toss them in the sugar, flour, a pinch of salt and a pinch of cinnamon. Arrange them in the part-cooked flan case. Pour the cream over the top and bake in a hot oven for 30–35 minutes. This is best served hot or warm.

CREAMY ONION SOUP

4 large onions
2 oz butter
1¾ pints beef stock
1 gill double cream
salt, pepper
grated cheese

Peel and thinly slice the onions. Heat the butter in a thick pan, and toss the onion slices in this until pale golden in colour. Add the stock, bring to the boil and allow to simmer for 1 hour. Liquidize, or press the mixture through a sieve. Season to taste, reheat and just before serving, add the cream and a sprinkling of grated cheese.

DUCK WITH CHERRIES

1–4 lb duckling
2 oranges
2 tbs brown sugar
2 tbs whisky or gin
salt, pepper
1 lb tin pitted morello cherries

Prick the duckling all over with a skewer. Cut 1 orange into quarters and place these inside the duck. Rub it well with salt and put it in a very hot oven for 10–15 minutes. Pour off the fat which will have gathered in the bottom of the roasting tin, and use this later, for sauté potatoes or pastry for a savoury pie. Reduce the oven heat to moderate. Spread the duck with a mixture of brown sugar and the grated rind of ½ orange. Season with salt and pepper and cook for a further 20 minutes. Baste with the juice of 1 orange and cook for a further 1–1½ hours, basting frequently. Pour off all the excess fat. Warm the whisky, pour it over the duck and ignite. Transfer the duck to a hot serving dish and keep it warm. Meanwhile pour the degreased duck gravy into a small pan. Add 2 tbs juice from the tin of cherries and allow to boil quickly for a few minutes. Blend in the cherries and allow to heat through. Serve this sauce with the duck. Because this method of cooking produces a moist, but not greasy duck, it is also excellent served cold. In this case, the sauce should be refrigerated, so that the fat will solidify on the surface and may be easily removed.

RISOTTO

½ lb Italian rice
salt, pepper
2 large onions
¼ lb mushrooms
2 large tomatoes
½ pint stock
1 bay leaf
2 oz butter
2 tbs oil

Heat the butter and oil together in a large pan. Add the peeled, sliced onion and allow to cook gently until soft, but not brown. Add the sliced mushrooms, rice, bay leaf, salt and pepper and stir well. Allow to cook for 5 minutes, stirring all the time, then add the tomatoes, peeled and roughly chopped. Stir well, then add the boiling stock. Allow to cook for 15–20 minutes, checking from time to time, in case more stock is needed. When the rice is cooked, all the liquid should be absorbed, leaving moist but not soggy, separate grains of rice.

WHIPPED CREAM ROLL

5 eggs
6 oz castor sugar
2 tbs brandy
3 tbs cocoa
1 tsp baking powder
½ pint double cream
icing sugar

Separate the eggs. Beat together the yolks and sugar until fluffy. Sift together the cocoa and baking powder and fold this into the egg yolks. Add the brandy. When well mixed fold in the stiffly beaten egg whites. Line a Swiss roll tin with greaseproof paper. Paint it lightly with oil, then pour in the mixture. Bake in a fairly low oven for 10 minutes. Peel off the paper and allow the cake to cool. When cool, but not absolutely cold, spread it with the whipped cream. Roll it up, wrap it in foil and chill in the refrigerator for at least 1 hour. Serve sprinkled with icing sugar.

PRAWN AND EGG MOUSSE

6 eggs
¼ pint cream
½ pint mayonnaise
1 clove garlic (optional)
½ oz gelatine
½ gill tomato juice
4 oz shelled prawns
1 tbs tomato purée
1 tsp Worcester sauce

Hardboil the eggs, and allow to cool. Shell and chop them finely. Soak the gelatine in the tomato juice for 10 minutes, then heat it gently until the gelatine has dissolved completely. Blend this tomato gelatine and the finely chopped eggs into the mayonnaise. Add the crushed clove of garlic, tomato purée and Worcester sauce. When quite cold, stir in the cream and prawns. Cover the inside of a soufflé mould with a light film of oil. Pour in the mousse mixture and chill for at least 2 hours before serving. Unmould on to a serving plate and decorate with twists of lemon, sprigs of watercress and a few black olives.

PORTUGUESE FILLET OF PORK

1 lb pork fillet
1 orange
2 tbs orange juice
2 tbs oil
½ gill white wine
salt, pepper
parsley
1 green pepper
½ oz butter
4 oz rice

Cut the pork into slices, discarding any fat or gristle. Flatten the slices with a steak mallet or rolling pin. Sprinkle them with salt and pepper and allow to stand for 3 hours. Boil the rice in salted water in the usual way. Heat the oil in a thick frying pan. Add the pork and fry quickly on both sides until golden brown. Add the orange juice and wine and allow to simmer for 5 minutes. Arrange the pork in the middle of a warm serving dish. Heat the juices in the pan, stirring in all the bits which have stuck to the sides. Surround the meat with the lightly buttered rice. Pour the sauce over the meat and garnish with thinly sliced peeled orange, and slivers of green pepper.

GRILLED GARLIC TOMATOES

4 large tomatoes
1 clove garlic
salt, pepper
parsley
2 tbs oil

Halve the tomatoes laterally. Make a few small incisions in the flesh of each tomato half. Rub in the crushed garlic, salt and pepper. Sprinkle with finely chopped parsley and oil. Allow to stand for 30 minutes, so that the flavours can mingle well. Grill until tender and lightly browned.

GREEK YOGURT

1¼ pints natural yogurt
4 tbs clear honey
3 tbs finely chopped almonds

Empty the yogurt into a glass serving dish. Just before serving, stir in the honey and almonds.

GRAPEFRUIT AND ORANGE SALAD

2 grapefruit
2 oranges
2 tbs clear honey

Halve the grapefruit and the oranges. Scoop out all the flesh, and cut it into small pieces, discarding any pith, seeds or skin. Keep the grapefruit halves for serving from. Pour the honey over the fruit and allow it to stand for 1 hour before serving chilled.

PROVENCAL BEEF STEW

2 lb topside of beef
1 lb onions
2 tomatoes
1 carrot
2 tbs oil
thyme
salt, pepper
1 wineglassful sherry
   or vermouth
2 oz black olives

Peel and slice the onions. Heat the oil in a thick pan. Add the sliced onions and cook until soft but not brown. Add the beef, and brown it quickly all over. Add the peeled and sliced tomatoes, carrot, salt, pepper and a sprig of thyme. Pour the sherry over the meat, cover, and cook in a very low oven for 4 hours. Half an hour before the meat is cooked, stir in the olives.

MACARONI MILANO

½ lb macaroni
½ pint beef stock
2 oz butter
2½ oz grated parmesan
   cheese
1½ oz grated gruyére
   cheese
salt, pepper

Have ready a large pan of salted, boiling water. Add the macaroni, broken into 1-inch pieces. Allow to boil for 10 minutes, then drain well. Put it in a second pan with the stock and allow to simmer until all the liquid has been absorbed. Stir in the gruyère cheese. Stir until that has melted, then add the butter and parmesan cheese. Remove from the heat, toss well and serve at once.

CHOCOLATE AND CHESTNUT

6 oz plain chocolate
6 oz unsalted butter
1 tbs rum
1 lb tinned sweetened
   chestnut purée
icing sugar

Melt the chocolate, either in a low oven or in a bowl over a pan of boiling water. Blend in the softened butter, chestnut purée and icing sugar to taste. Blend in the rum. Transfer the mixture to a serving dish—I find that a long, tray-like dish is best—and chill before serving. This is a very rich pudding and should be served with thin cream which, surprisingly, makes it seem less gooey.

TOMATO AND ORANGE SOUP

2 lb tomatoes
1 tsp sugar
1 orange
½ lemon
salt, pepper
1 wineglassful sherry or
    vermouth

Skin the tomatoes, by plunging them into boiling water for a moment. Halve them, liquidize them, then press them through a sieve. To the resulting tomato juice add the juice of the orange and the juice of ½ lemon. Blend in the sherry or vermouth, sugar, salt and pepper. Serve either hot or chilled.

LAMB FRICASSEE WITH LETTUCE

3 lb shoulder of lamb
4 oz butter
1 lettuce
1 bunch spring onions
salt, pepper
1 gill stock or water
2 tbs chopped fresh
    or dried dill
1 lemon
2 egg yolks

Dice the meat, trimming it of fat and gristle. Heat the butter in a large, thick pan, and add the meat. Toss it until brown all over, then add the chopped spring onions, including some of the green part. Season well with salt and pepper, and add the boiling stock or water. Allow to simmer gently for 30 minutes, then add the washed and sliced lettuce leaves, dill and more liquid if necessary. Cover the pan and allow to simmer very gently for about 1 hour, or until the meat is very tender. Beat together the egg yolks and 3–4 tablespoonfuls of lemon juice. Gradually add the strained sauce from the pan to this egg and lemon mixture. Whisk well and stir it over a low flame until it thickens, but do not allow it to boil. Pour this sauce over the meat and lettuce before serving.

SPROUTS WITH WALNUTS

2 lb small sprouts
1½ oz butter
salt, pepper
2 oz walnuts

Wash the sprouts well, discarding the outer leaves. Allow the sprouts to soak in lukewarm salted water for 10 minutes. Drain well, rinse in cold water, then plunge the sprouts into fast boiling salted water for 10 minutes. Drain them well. Heat the butter in a pan. Add the drained sprouts and roughly chopped walnuts, and toss well for 5 minutes before serving.

APPLE OMELETTE

6 eggs
1 oz castor sugar
2 dess double cream
½ lemon
1 oz butter
4 tbs apple purée

Whisk together the eggs and sugar. Stir in the finely grated rind of ½ lemon and the cream. Mix well. Heat the butter in an omelette pan and when completely melted, pour in the batter. Stir the centre of the omelette until it begins to set. Lift the edges of the omelette to allow any uncooked mixture to run underneath. Place the apple purée in the centre of the omelette, then fold it into three. Slide it on to a sugared plate and sprinkle with more sugar before serving very hot.

TOMATO MOUSSE

6 large tomatoes
1 oz butter
1 small onion
2 oz mushrooms
1 clove
1 tsp sugar
salt, pepper
fresh tarragon or basil
Worcester sauce
gelatine
double cream

Skin and roughly chop the tomatoes. Heat the butter in a frying pan. Add the tomatoes, chopped onion, sliced mushrooms, cloves, sugar, salt, pepper and a few leaves of fresh tarragon or basil. Allow to simmer gently until the whole mixture is soft enough to be pressed through a sieve. Check the seasoning, and blend in 1 tsp Worcester sauce. Measure the resulting tomato purée. For every 1 pint of purée use ½ oz gelatine. Dissolve it in boiling water, then stir it into the purée. When it begins to set, blend in whipped cream, in the proportion of 5 fl oz per 1 pint purée. Make sure that it is so well blended that no streaks of cream remain. Pour it into a mould and chill for at least 2 hours before serving.

MEDAILLONS IN MANDELROCK

2 veal chops
2 pork chops
salt, pepper
nutmeg
1 egg
5 oz almonds
butter
oil

Trim the chops of all skin and fat. Cut the meat into finger-thick slices. Beat them lightly and season them with salt, pepper and a little grated nutmeg. Coat them with beaten egg. Finely chop the skinned almonds. Coat the meat slices with the chopped almonds, pressing them in firmly with the blade of a knife. Fry them in a mixture of oil and butter, taking care that the almonds do not become too brown.

CARROTS WITH PARSLEY SAUCE

1½ lb new carrots
salt, pepper
2 oz butter
4 tbs flour
4 tbs finely chopped
  parsley
1 pint chicken stock
salt, pepper

Wash, but do not peel the carrots. Boil them in salted water until tender. The time of cooking will depend on the size of the carrots, of course, but do not allow them to become too soft. Meanwhile, prepare a parsley sauce. Melt the butter in a pan. Sprinkle in the flour and allow to cook for 1–2 minutes, stirring all the time. The flour must not be allowed to colour. Gradually add the hot stock, stirring all the time. Stir over a gentle heat until the sauce comes to the boil, then allow it to simmer for 10 minutes, still stirring frequently. Season to taste with salt, pepper and the parsley. Drain the cooked, whole carrots and arrange them in a serving dish. Coat them with the hot parsley sauce.

ALMOND APPLES

1 lb Bramley apples
2 oz ground almonds
2 oz soft brown sugar
1½ oz butter

Peel, core and slice the apples. Place them in an ovenware dish. Sprinkle them with brown sugar, ground almonds and nuts of butter. Bake in a moderate oven for 30 minutes. Serve with cream.

EGGS WITH DILL SAUCE

4 eggs
1 small onion
1 oz butter
1 dess chopped parsley
2 tbs chopped dill
1 tbs flour
1 gill stock
½ lemon
1 gill sour cream
salt, pepper
sugar

Hardboil the eggs. Meanwhile, heat the butter in a pan and add the finely chopped peeled onion. Fry until soft but not brown. Stir in the parsley and 1 tbs dill. (Fresh dill is not always easy to find, but dried dill will do quite well.) Sprinkle in the flour, stir well, cook for 2–3 minutes, then gradually add the stock, lemon juice, a pinch of sugar, salt and pepper. Allow to cook gently for 10 minutes, stirring all the time, then remove from the heat and stir in the remaining dill and sour cream. Check the seasoning. Shell the hardboiled eggs and add them to the dill sauce. Reheat gently, without allowing to boil.

STUFFED KIDNEYS

10 lamb's kidneys
4 oz butter
1 clove garlic
thyme
parsley
½ tsp dry mustard
salt, pepper
2 tbs breadcrumbs
2 tbs mango chutney
½ tsp Worcester sauce
1 tbs redcurrant jelly

Skin the kidneys. Split them in half, without completely severing them. Blend together all the other ingredients. Put a spoonful of this savoury mixture into each split kidney. Place them on a greased tray and cook in a hot oven for 10–15 minutes. As the stuffing melts, creating a lot of delicious sauce, serve creamed potatoes or rice with this dish.

FRIED ONION RINGS

7–8 large onions
salt, pepper
3 tbs flour
oil for frying
paprika

Peel the onions and cut them into thin rings. Sprinkle them with plenty of salt and allow to stand in a colander for 20 minutes. Dry them well in kitchen paper. Put the flour, salt and pepper in a large plastic bag. Add the onion rings and toss well, until each ring is well coated with flour. Heat a panful of deep oil, and when very hot, add the floured onion rings. Allow to fry for 5 minutes, then remove them from the oil. Reheat the oil until it starts to smoke. Plunge in the onions a second time, and fry until crisp and golden. Drain on kitchen paper before serving sprinkled with paprika.

STUFFED ORANGES

4 large oranges
1 apple
1 tbs raisins
1 oz walnuts
1 oz castor sugar

Halve the oranges. With a sharp grapefruit knife scoop out the flesh. Cut it into small pieces, discarding any pips or pith. Blend in the raisins, finely grated apple, grated nuts and sugar. Mix well. Return this mixture to each of the empty orange halves,* and serve with whipped cream.

*To make the orange halves balance more safely, you may need to slice a small sliver of skin from the base of each.

PEA SOUP WITH BACON

1 lb dried peas
4 rashers bacon
1 large onion
salt, pepper
Worcester sauce
3 pints beef or chicken
    stock
1 oz butter

Soak the peas overnight. Dice the bacon. Heat the butter in a thick pan. Add the bacon and toss it lightly until brown. Add the peeled, sliced onion and cook until golden. Add the drained peas, salt, pepper and boiling stock. Allow to cook, covered, for 2 hours. Just before serving add a dash of Worcester sauce and a little cream, if liked.

ESCALOPES DE VEAU EN AILLADE

4 veal escalopes
4 cloves garlic
1 lb tomatoes
oil
½ cupful dry bread-
    crumbs
salt, pepper
parsley

Cover the bottom of a thick pan with oil. Heat it, and when hot, but not boiling, add the seasoned escalopes. Cook gently until just golden on both sides. Add the skinned and chopped tomatoes, and as soon as they have softened, add the breadcrumbs, crushed garlic and plenty of finely chopped parsley. Cook for a further 8–10 minutes.

ONIONS TOPPED WITH CREAM

1½ lb small onions
3 oz butter
½ gill double cream
salt, pepper

Peel the onions, and allow them to soak in cold, salted water for 1 hour. Drain them well, plunge them into boiling water and allow to boil for 15 minutes. Drain again, and immediately plunge into fresh boiling, salted water. Allow to cook until the onions are soft but not falling apart. Drain them well, and arrange in a serving dish. Heat the butter and pour this over the onions. Sprinkle with plenty of freshly ground black pepper. Heat the cream and pour this over the onions before serving.

RHUBARB SPONGE

1 lb cold, stewed rhubarb
3 oz butter
5 oz flour
2 tbs milk
1 egg
2 oz castor sugar
salt

Place the rhubarb in the bottom of a buttered pie dish. Cream together the butter and sugar. Add the beaten egg, a pinch of salt, then gradually sift in the flour, stirring well between each addition. If the mixture is too thick, blend in a little cold milk. Beat well for 2 minutes, then cover the fruit with this mixture and bake in a hot oven for 20–30 minutes. Serve either hot or cold.

TUNA AND ALMOND SALAD

8 oz tinned tuna fish
3 oz flaked almonds
2 eggs
2 oz black olives
3 sticks celery
1½ gills mayonnaise
salt, pepper
lemon juice

Hardboil the eggs. Drain the oil from the fish. Flake the fish and blend in the diced hardboiled eggs, chopped celery, chopped, stoned olives and almonds cut into slivers. Fold in the mayonnaise, and season with salt, pepper and lemon juice.

FILET DE BOEUF FLAMBE A L'AVIGNONNAISE

4 fillet steaks
salt, pepper
1 clove garlic
3 oz butter
1½ tbs brandy
4 thick slices French
  bread

Rub the steaks with crushed garlic. Spread some salt and coarsely ground black pepper on a plate. Roll each steak in this. Heat 1 oz butter in a thick frying pan, and cook the steaks on both sides until very brown. Add a further 1 oz butter and as soon as this has melted, pour the warmed brandy over the steaks and set it alight. The flames will die down, then allow the steaks to cook for a further ½ minute. Meanwhile, fry the slices of bread in the remaining butter. Serve each steak atop a piece of fried French bread, and pour the juices over.

LEEKS AND MUSHROOMS

2 lb leeks
½ lb mushrooms
2 oz butter
salt, pepper
1 gill tomato juice

Wash the leeks carefully. Slice them, using only the white parts. Heat the butter in a thick pan, add the leeks and allow to cook quickly for 4–5 minutes. Add the sliced mushrooms and fry for a further 4–5 minutes. Season with salt and pepper, and pour over the tomato juice. Cover and allow to simmer for 10–15 minutes, or until the leeks are quite soft.

EASTERN ORANGES

6 large oranges
1 oz almond nibs
4 oz stoned dates
½ gill brandy
1 gill orange juice

Peel the oranges and thinly slice them, discarding any pith or pips. Put them in a serving bowl, together with the almond nibs and finely chopped stoned dates. Stir in the brandy and orange juice and allow to stand in a cool place for at least 1 hour, before serving with whipped, brandy-flavoured cream.

AVOCADO AND PRAWN MAYONNAISE

2 avocado pears
6 oz peeled prawns
½ pint mayonnaise
2 tbs tomato ketchup
1 tbs double cream
Worcester sauce
½ lemon

Halve the avocado pears and discard the stones. Sprinkle each half with lemon juice. Fill the cavity in each half with prawns. Blend together the mayonnaise, ketchup, cream and a dash of Worcester sauce. Pour this over the prawns.

LAMB CUTLETS WITH MINT BUTTER

8 lamb cutlets
2 oz butter
salt, pepper
lemon juice
mint

Pound a handful of mint leaves in a mortar. Blend in the softened butter, salt, pepper and a few drops of fresh lemon juice. Score the cutlets lightly on both sides with a knife. Coat them with the butter, also on both sides. Allow to stand for 1 hour before grilling. The cutlets should be turned very frequently during cooking.

CHICORY WITH CHEESE SAUCE

8 pieces chicory
salt, pepper
½ pint cheese sauce
2 oz fresh white bread-crumbs
2 oz grated parmesan cheese
1 oz butter

Trim the outer leaves from the chicory. Have ready a pan of boiling salted water. Add the chicory and allow it to cook until almost tender. Drain it well, then arrange it in a fireproof dish. Cover it with the cheese sauce—just a basic white sauce with cream and grated cheese added. Sprinkle with the breadcrumbs and parmesan, mixed together. Dot with nuts of butter and bake in a moderate oven for 30 minutes.

GOOSEBERRY ICE CREAM

1 lb gooseberries
4 oz sugar
1 gill double cream

Put the gooseberries and sugar in a pan, without topping and tailing them. Steam them until quite soft, then press through a sieve. Allow the purée to cool, then blend in the whipped cream. Pour this mixture into an ice-making tray, cover it with foil and freeze at maximum temperature for 2½–3 hours, agitating the mixture twice, with a fork, during the freezing period.

TOMATOED PRAWNS

1 oz butter
1 small onion
½ lb tomatoes
½ lb peeled prawns or
  shrimps
2 tbs double cream
1 cupful mayonnaise
salt, pepper
cayenne pepper

Melt the butter. Peel and finely chop the onion and fry it gently in the butter until soft but not brown. Add the skinned and chopped tomatoes and allow to simmer for 5 minutes. Add the prawns or shrimps. Season with salt, pepper and a dash of cayenne pepper. Remove from the heat and when cool blend in the cream and mayonnaise. Serve in glasses on a bed of shredded lettuce, or in scooped-out and toasted bridge rolls.

HOTPOT

2 lb shoulder beef
1 lb best end neck
  of lamb
2 large onions
2 lb potatoes
flour
salt, pepper
beef or chicken stock

Cut the meat into fairly large pieces. Toss them in seasoned flour. Place them in the bottom of a hotpot, or large ovenware casserole, together with the peeled and thinly sliced onions. Cover level with stock and season well with salt and pepper. Cover with a lid and allow to cook in a moderate oven for 1½ hours. Peel the potatoes and cut them into irregular, knobbly pieces, Stir them into the meat and onions, making sure that some of the knobbly pieces are at the top. Season again with salt and pepper, cover with a lid and allow to cook for a further 1½ hours, removing the lid for the final 10 minutes. Pickled red cabbage is the traditional accompaniment to this dish.

SPINACH WITH CHEESE

1 lb spinach
salt, pepper
2 oz butter
2 oz grated parmesan
  cheese
nutmeg

Wash the spinach thoroughly. Heat 1 oz butter in a large pan. Season it with salt and pepper. Drain as much water as possible from the spinach leaves, then add them to the hot butter. Stir well, cover the pan and allow to cook for 10–15 minutes, pressing down the spinach leaves with a spoon from time to time. Just before serving, stir in the remaining 1 oz butter and the grated parmesan. Stir well and serve very hot.

APPLE FLAN

1 lb Bramley apples
4 oz sugar
½ lemon
cinnamon
2 oz butter
2 oz flaked almonds
3 tbs apricot jam
½ lb short pastry

Peel, core and slice the apples. Cook them slowly in a saucepan, together with the sugar, butter, grated rind and juice of ½ lemon, apricot jam and a pinch of ground cinnamon. Cook very gently, stirring all the time. When almost cooked, stir in the almonds. Line a flan ring with short pastry. Pour in the mixture and bake in a moderate oven for 45 minutes.

PARSNIP MAYONNAISE

3 medium parsnips
½ pint mayonnaise
lettuce
watercress

Trim, but do not peel the parsnips. Boil them in salted water until tender. Allow to cool, then skin and slice them. Arrange the parsnip slices on a bed of shredded lettuce and sprigs of watercress. Coat with plenty of mayonnaise.

ROAST PORK WITH LEMON

2½ lb leg of pork
1 lemon
salt, pepper
flour
2 lb potatoes
3 oz olive oil

Rub the meat well with the juice of ½ lemon. Season it with salt and pepper. Sprinkle it lightly with flour and place it in a roasting tray. Peel the potatoes, season them with salt and pepper and surround the joint with them. Spoon the oil and the juice of ½ lemon over the meat and potatoes. Cook in a moderate oven for 2 hours.

CABBAGE WITH CARAWAY

1 medium white cabbage
salt, pepper
2 oz butter
2 tbs caraway seeds
1 gill chicken stock

Shred the cabbage quite finely, discarding the outer leaves. Heat the butter in a pan. Add the shredded cabbage and toss well. Stir in the caraway seeds, salt and freshly ground black pepper. Allow to cook for 5 minutes, stirring all the time, then add the boiling stock. Cover the pan and allow to cook for a further 10 minutes. Drain well before serving.

STUFFED PRUNES

1 lb large prunes
½ pint fresh orange juice
1 oz sugar
3 oz whole almonds

Soak the prunes overnight in sufficient water to barely cover them. Cook them in the same water, together with the sugar, until tender and until very little juice remains. Allow them to cool, then carefully remove the stones with a sharp-pointed knife. Skin the almonds by pouring boiling water over them, then cold water, after which the skins may be easily rubbed off. Insert an almond in place of each prune stone. Arrange them in a wide saucepan or frying pan, in a single layer. Pour the orange juice over them, and allow to simmer gently for 10 minutes. Transfer them carefully to a serving dish and sprinkle with any remaining skinned almonds. Allow the orange juice to cook for a further 2–3 minutes, then pour it over the prunes. Allow to cool, then chill, before serving with cream.

ORANGED MELON

1 Honeydew melon or
  4 tiny Ogen melons
2 oranges

If you use a honeydew melon, slice off its top, and carefully scoop out all the flesh, discarding the seeds. Cut the flesh into cubes, and cover them with the juice of 2 oranges and the grated rind of 1 orange. Return the oranged melon cubes to the scooped-out melon, wrap it carefully in a polythene bag and chill for at least 2 hours before serving. If you are using the individual Ogen melons, halve them and scoop out the flesh, then continue in the same way as for the honeydew.

CHICKEN AND AUBERGINE CASSEROLE

1 medium-sized roasting
  chicken
3 cloves garlic
4 aubergines
2 onions
2 oz butter
3 green peppers
salt, pepper
1 lb tin tomatoes

Peel and slice the onions. Heat the butter in a thick frying pan. Add the crushed garlic and sliced onions and cook gently until tender, but not brown. Transfer the onions to an ovenware casserole. Cut the chicken into 4–6 joints. Toss them in the butter, over a high flame, until brown all over, then arrange them on top of the onion layer in the casserole dish. Fry the sliced aubergines and peppers, and arrange these on top of the chicken. Season well with salt and pepper. Pour over the contents of a 1 lb tin of tomatoes. Cover with a lid and cook in a low oven for 2 hours.

SWISS POTATOES

2 lb potatoes
gros sel (coarse sea salt)
3 oz butter

Scrub the potatoes, but do not peel them. Boil them in salted water until almost cooked. Peel and slice them thinly. Heat the butter in a thick frying pan. Add the potatoes, arranged in a thick layer. Season well with gros sel. Cover the pan and cook over a very low flame until the bottom of the potato layer is crisp and golden. Turn the potatoes carefully. Cover again, and cook until all the outside is crisp, and the inside soft and creamy.

CHEESECAKE

1 lb cottage or curd
  cheese
2 oz butter
3 oz castor sugar
2 oz currants or sultanas
2 eggs
cinnamon
nutmeg
2 tbs brandy
2 tbs double cream
½ lb sweet short pastry

Line a flan ring with short pastry and bake it blind, for 30 minutes in a moderate oven. Allow it to cool. Beat the eggs and stir them into the cheese, mixing well. Add the softened butter and beat well, then blend in the cream. Beat this mixture for about 5 minutes, then add the brandy, sugar, currants and a pinch of grated nutmeg and powdered cinnamon. Pour this mixture into the flan case and bake for 30 minutes in a moderate oven. Serve cold.

LETTUCE AND ONION SOUP

2 oz butter
1 large onion
1 large lettuce
2 pints chicken stock
salt, pepper
½ gill double cream

Heat the butter in a thick pan, and fry the finely chopped onion in this until soft, without allowing it to colour. Add the shredded lettuce and allow to cook for a few minutes, then add the boiling stock, salt, and pepper. Bring to the boil, cover and allow to simmer for 5–7 minutes. Liquidize, or rub the mixture through a sieve. Reheat, remove from the flame and blend in the cream just before serving.

COD PROVENCALE

1½ lb middle cut of cod
2 onions
1 clove garlic
1 lb tomatoes
4 oz black olives
sage, thyme
parsley
1 gill olive oil
flour
salt, pepper

Cut the fish into 2-inch squares, discarding any skin or bones. Heat the oil in a large frying pan. Toss the fish squares in seasoned flour then fry them quickly until golden brown all over and thoroughly cooked. Transfer to a serving dish and keep warm. Reduce the heat under the frying pan and cook the peeled, sliced onions and finely chopped garlic gently for 5 minutes. Add the peeled, skinned and quartered tomatoes and stoned olives, and cook gently for a further 3 minutes. Spoon this mixture over the fish before serving, sprinkled with chopped fresh sage, thyme and parsley.

RAW MUSHROOM SALAD

¾ lb button mushrooms
2 tbs finely chopped
   parsley
1 clove garlic
salt, pepper
6 tbs olive oil
2 tbs lemon juice

Slice the mushrooms into a plastic container with an airtight lid. Add the parsley. Whisk together the oil, lemon juice, salt pepper and crushed garlic. Pour this over the mushrooms and parsley. Mix weil, and cover with the lid. Allow the mushrooms to marinade in this dressing for 2 hours, turning the container upside down from time to time, to ensure even distribution of the dressing. Serve cold.

BANANA TRIFLE

1 chocolate Swiss Roll
3 ripe bananas
4 eggs
1 pint milk
2 oz castor sugar
1 gill double cream

Slice the Swiss Roll, and put it in the bottom of a deep serving dish. Cover with the sliced bananas. Beat the eggs and sugar. Gradually add the boiling milk, whisking all the time. Return the mixture to the pan and reheat it gently without allowing it to boil. If you are unsure of your ability to do this, it might be wiser to use a double saucepan. Stir the custard with a wooden spoon until it thickens enough to coat the spoon. Pour this custard over the banana and Swiss Roll. Allow to cool and set. Top with a layer of whipped cream, and decorate with chopped nuts, glacé cherries, angelica, etc.

EGG AND TOMATO MAYONNAISE

4 eggs
4 large tomatoes
½ pint mayonnaise

Hardboil the eggs. Cool, shell and carefully slice them. Turn the tomatoes upside down and slice them downwards, without actually severing them. Insert a slice of egg between each slice of tomato, so that it looks like a red and white flower. Serve the mayonnaise separately.

CHICKEN WITH ORANGE

1 roasting chicken
1 large orange
1 large onion
chicken stock
1 oz flour
salt, pepper
2 tbs oil
4 oz button mushrooms
parsley

Joint the chicken. Put the flour, salt and pepper in a plastic bag, and toss the chicken pieces in this until well coated. Keep the remaining flour. Heat the oil in a frying pan, and fry the floured chicken pieces in this until golden all over. Transfer them to a casserole dish. Fry the finely chopped onion in the oil until lightly browned. Stir in the remaining flour from the bag and allow to cook for 2–3 minutes, stirring all the time. Halve and squeeze the orange. Make the orange juice up to 1 pint by adding chicken stock. Gradually add this to the onion and flour mixture, stirring well. Bring to the boil, and pour this over the chicken. Stir in the sliced mushrooms. Carefully remove the pith from the squeezed orange halves. Cut the peel into thin strips. Stir half of them into the chicken, cover with a lid and cook in a fairly low oven for 1½ hours. Just before serving, stir in the remaining strips of orange peel and some finely chopped parsley.

CARROT PUREE

1½ lb carrots
3 oz butter
salt, pepper
1 gill double cream
1 tsp sugar
1 medium onion

Peel the carrots and slice them. Peel and slice the onion. Boil the carrots and onion together in salted water until soft enough to be liquidized, or pressed through a sieve. Stir in the butter, cream and sugar and a sprinkling of freshly ground black pepper. Reheat gently before serving.

BROWN BREAD CREAM

4 egg yolks
2 oz castor sugar
¾ pint milk
1 tbs sherry
1 gill double cream
2 oz fresh brown bread-
  crumbs

Whisk together the egg yolks and sugar. Put them in the top of a double pan. Gradually add the hot milk, stirring all the time. Allow to cook gently until thick enough to coat the spoon. Add the brandy and allow to cool. When cool but not quite cold, fold in the whipped cream and breadcrumbs. Chill well.

Index